Best of the Best
from
Hawai'i
Cookbook

Selected Recipes from Hawai'i's
FAVORITE COOKBOOKS

Kaua'i

Ni'ihau

O'ahu

Honolulu

Moloka'i

Lana'i

Maui

Kaho'olawe

The Hawaiian
Islands

Hawai'i

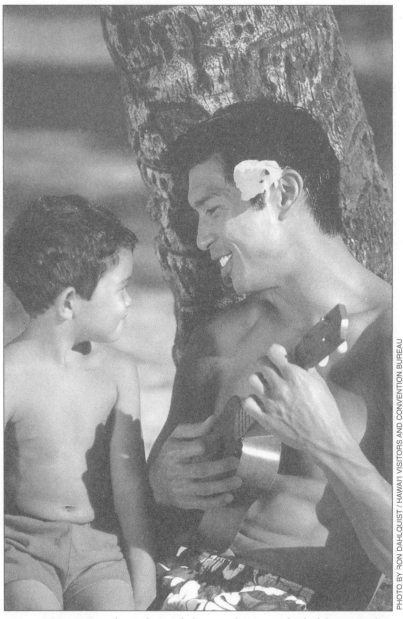

Since 1970, visitors have descended upon the Annual Ukulele Festival at the Kapiolani Park Bandstand in Waikiki for a free concert showcasing the finest ukulele players in the world. The ukulele is Hawai'i's most popular musical instrument.

Best of the Best from

Hawaii

Cookbook

Selected Recipes from Hawai'i's
FAVORITE COOKBOOKS

Edited by
Gwen McKee
and
Barbara Moseley

QUAIL RIDGE PRESS
Preserving America's Food Heritage

Copyright ©2014 by Quail Ridge Press, Inc.
ISBN-13: 978-1-938879-03-6

First printing, September 2014

Front cover: Kalalau Valley, Kaua'i, ©Ron Dahlquist, Hawai'i Visitors & Convention Bureau
Back cover photo by Greg Campbell • Illustrations by Tupper England
Printed in South Korea

QUAIL RIDGE PRESS
P. O. Box 123 • Brandon, MS 39043 • 1-800-343-1583
info@quailridge.com • www.quailridge.com • facebook.com/cookbookladies

Contents

PHOTO COURTESY GWEN McKEE

Every Wednesday and Saturday at the Hilo Farmers' Market, one can find an amazing variety of isle fruits, vegetables, coffees, herbs and spices, as well as beautiful orchids and other flowers and plants. And there are crafts, too. Editor Gwen McKee enjoyed sampling and learning, and was as much impressed with the friendly people as with the exotic produce.

Preface

Paradise. Hawaiʻi IS paradise! It is one of the most beautiful places on earth. I have to admit that traveling to Hawaiʻi to research this BEST OF THE BEST state cookbook was *not* a tedious task. The locals helped us everywhere we went.

In Mililani on Oʻahu, Steve told us of the wonderful food-related traditions and customs that are unique to Hawaiʻi. Jeff, whose company is the largest distributor of Hawaiian cookbooks, was a gold mine of information. He and his associate, Bennett, took an entire afternoon off from their busy schedules to provide us with valuable suggestions, recommendations, and directions in our pursuit. They explained that the food of the islands was four things: Pacific Rim (Asian-American); Hawaiian Regional (Pacific Rim with Hawaiian touches); ethnic cooking from five or six nationalities; and local cooking, which is somewhat of a mix of all of that, but not fancy.

On the big island, Shirley's little coffee shop in Hilo was a delight. Under the banyan trees, we shared coffee, muffins, and wonderful stories. On Saturday, the Farmers Market gave us the chance to taste and see fascinating local fruits and vegetables.

At Waimea Canyon, Joyce recognized me from having seen me on QVC. She raved about specific Hawaiian dishes, including likikoʻi cheesecake, which we later had—it was superb!

On Maui, we opted for adventure. After a lūʻau and little sleep, we watched a beautiful sunrise at 10,000 feet atop Mt. Haleakala, after which we rode bikes 38 miles down to the beach. That same evening we watched—this time relaxed with champagne—an equally incredible sunset aboard a smooth-sailing catamaran—our unforgettable sunrise/sunset day.

On the North Shore of Oʻahu, we thanked Irene for allowing us to share her famous shrimp recipe in this book; she wrote it down on a brown paper bag between waiting on customers in her umbrella-tabled yard near her yellow Shrimp Shack truck. The sign said, "Suck, peel, dip, eat." We did . . . yum, yum, yum!

We were very impressed with the people we encountered all over the Hawaiian Islands, particularly admiring the respect and reverence they have for their elders. Hula dancers can be young, old, big, or tiny—it doesn't matter. Their commonalities are their grace,

When researching Hawaiian Cookbooks, lovely Faith at the Kaua'i Marriott Resort, brought many for me to see at 6:30 the next morning . . . a beautiful example of how friendly and out-reaching Hawaiians are all over the islands.

and their smiles, and their Hawaiian spirit. They exemplify the true meaning and spirit of aloha. You just want to hug them all.

Like the islands themselves, Hawaiian cooking can be an adventure as well. *Best of the Best from Hawai'i* has recipes that are more diverse, exotic, and different from other books in the BEST OF THE BEST STATE COOKBOOK SERIES. Don't hesitate to use your imagination, and to substitute similar ingredients you can find locally.

Beyond these selected recipes collected here, we are pleased to share a few of our favorite photographs and facts about Hawai'i. Did you know that all the islands were formed by volcanoes, some of which are still active? And that aloha means hello and goodbye? And that it's practically impossible to find a license plate that doesn't say Hawai'i?

We are proud to share information on the sixty-one Hawaiian cookbooks that were selected to contribute recipes to this collection (see page 165).

We wish to thank food editors; bookstore, gift shop, café, and restaurant managers; the personnel at tourist bureaus and chambers; museums and state offices who helped us with information and photographs; and especially all the great Hawaiian cooks who created and developed and shared their recipes. *Mahalo nui loa* (thank you very much).

Aloha,
Gwen McKee and Barbara Moseley

Beverages and Appetizers

The natural phenomenon Spouting Horn, in Kaua'i, sprays salt water fifty feet into the air. The spray is created when the surf forces water into a lava tube and into the air through a small opening at the surface. At sunset the spray becomes incandescent with the colors of the rainbow.

Café à la Queen of Tonga

Queen Halaevalu Mata'aho, descendant to the throne of Tonga after five hundred years of royalty, was the honored guest for the two-day opening celebration festivities of the Waiākea Village Resort in Hilo, along with her daughter Princess Pilolevu Tuku'aho. In the Queen's honor, Don the Beachcomber concocted the following:

½ cup whipping cream	2 teaspoons coconut syrup*
¼ teaspoon instant coffee	8 ounces hot Kona coffee
½ teaspoon cocoa	½ ounce gold rum
1 drop almond extract	1 Tahitian vanilla bean
1 light dusting of cinnamon	

Blend whipping cream, instant coffee, cocoa, almond extract, and cinnamon until granules of coffee dissolve. Whip until stiff peaks form. Into a large cup or glass, add coconut syrup and coffee, and stir until the syrup dissolves. Add rum. Top with a generous dollop of the spiced whipped cream. Add Tahitian vanilla bean and gently stir.

Note: For best results, use Hana Bay Premium Gold Rum.

*A syrup made from coconut milk and sugar. It can be bought in 12-ounce jars.

Hawai'i Tropical Rum Drinks & Cuisine

Donn Beach, best known as Don the Beachcomber, is considered to have single-handedly transformed the hospitality industry in Hawai'i in the 1940s and 1950s through his creation of the International Market Place with its famous Treehouse restaurant, his reformation of the Lahaina Historic District, and his successful Polynesian-theme restaurants, bars, and lū'au. Donn invented more than 90 tropical drinks, including the Zombie, Missionary's Downfall, and the Beachcomber's Daiquiri. The Zombie was considered the most lethal tropical drink ever created, and customers in Donn's bar were limited to two. To protect his recipes, Donn wrote them in code, and his bartenders had to follow coded symbols for the ingredients.

Hawaiian Coffee

10 drops almond extract
½ cup crème de cacao
1 cup sugar
½ cup cocoa
1 teaspoon salt

1 pint whipping cream
3 trays coffee ice cubes made
with Kona coffee (sweetened,
if desired)

Simmer almond extract, crème de cacao, sugar, cocoa, and salt until well blended. Refrigerate. Whip cream until firm, but not stiff. Fold into coffee mixture. When ready to serve, put ice cubes in punch bowl. Pour in chilled coffee mixture. Makes 30 servings.

Hawaii–Cooking with Aloha

Frosted Hawaiian Coffee

2 cups strong Kona coffee,
chilled
1 cup chilled pineapple juice

1 pint vanilla or coffee ice
cream, softened

Combine all ingredients; beat until smooth and foamy. Pour into tall glasses to serve. Serves 4–5.

The Tastes and Tales of Moiliili

Country Club Iced Tea

Almost every country club in Hawai'i (and some restaurants) make a version of this tea. The trick is to make it with plain ol' black tea, then add fruit juice and lots of fresh mint. Sometimes the juice is pineapple, sometimes it comes from an abundance of lemon trees in the backyard. One kama'āina family made a simple syrup by cooking the sugar first, thereby making it easier to dissolve. There is now a commercial version sold in cans. But fresh is still best.

½ gallon water
12 black tea bags
3 sprigs fresh mint
2 cups sugar

12 ounces pineapple juice
6 ounces lemon juice
Pineapple spears and fresh
mint sprigs for garnish

In a large pot, bring water to a boil. Steep the tea bags and fresh mint in the hot water. Remove the mint after 3 minutes, but continue to steep the tea until it is very dark. Remove tea bags. Add sugar and juices while tea is still warm. Stir to dissolve sugar. Pour into a gallon container and add water to fill. Refrigerate. Serve with ice and garnishes.

Hawaiian Country Tables

Fruit Punch

1 cup grenadine
½ cup lemon juice
1 cup strong tea
1 cup orange juice

1 cup pineapple juice
1 bottle maraschino cherries
Sugar or sugar syrup to taste
Mineral water (optional)

Combine all, sweetening to taste, and add mineral water, if desired. Serve cold.

How to Use Hawaiian Fruit

King Kalākaua's Champagne Punch

6 bottles champagne, divided
2 bottles Sauterne (white Bordeaux wine, not too dry or heavy)
6 lemons, sliced
6 oranges, sliced

6 mint leaves
1 ripe pineapple, peeled and sliced into sticks
1 cup sugar
2 cups brandy
2 quarts fresh strawberries

Chill bottles of champagne and Sauterne 5 hours or overnight.

Into a large punch bowl, add sliced lemons, sliced oranges, mint leaves, pineapple sticks, and sugar. Pour Sauterne and 3 bottles of the champagne into the ingredients in the punch bowl, and stir until sugar dissolves. Add brandy and fresh strawberries; mix gently. Before serving, add remaining 3 bottles of champagne.

Courtesy of Daughters of Hawaii
The Friends of 'Iolani Palace Cookbook

King David Kalākaua was known as the "Merrie Monarch" because he was solely responsible for the resurgence in Hawaiian culture and arts including the hula, which had been banned by missionaries. Each year the Merrie Monarch Festival, considered the world's most prestigious hula contest, is held in his honor.

Tiki Punch

If you are having a small enough party, delight your guests with their own "pineapple glass." When you hollow out the pineapple, take care not to cut through the skin. Use the pineapple for other dishes. It's also a great opportunity to experiment with different garnishes. Recipe serves one.

1 pineapple per guest
 or couple
1 ounce vodka
½ ounce Galliano liqueur

5 ounces orange juice
5 ounces pineapple juice
Champagne

Combine vodka, Galliano, and juices in a pitcher. Pour into pineapple, approximately ⅔ from the top. Fill with champagne and add garnishes.

Hawaii's Best Tropical Food & Drinks

Mai Tai

There is much discussion about the origin of the delightful Mai Tai. Whoever invented it, the Mai Tai has become one of the most popular drinks in the islands.

2 ounces light rum
1 ounce dark rum
1 ounce Triple Sec orange
 liqueur

½ ounce amaretto
½ ounce lime juice
Crushed ice

Mix the rums, Triple Sec, amaretto, and lime juice in a 7-ounce glass. Add crushed ice and garnish.

Hawaii's Best Tropical Food & Drinks

The origin of the Mai Tai has been debated for decades. Both Donn Beach (Don the Beachcomber) and Victor Bergerson (Trader Vic) claimed to have invented this tropical drink. Even though Trader Vic has been given the most credit, the truth may have gone to the grave with both men.

Macadamia Cheese Ball

1 pound Cheddar cheese,
  grated
1 (8-ounce) package cream
  cheese, softened
⅓ cup chopped sweet pickles
1 tablespoon Dijon mustard

2 tablespoons mayonnaise
2 tablespoons dry sherry
Dash of cayenne pepper
½ cup chopped macadamia
  nuts

Mix Cheddar cheese with softened cream cheese. Add pickles,
mustard, mayonnaise, and sherry. Form into ball, sprinkle with
cayenne pepper, and refrigerate. Roll in macadamia nuts before
serving. Serve with crackers. May keep refrigerated for up to 2
weeks.

Hilo Woman's Club Cookbook

Spam and Mushroom Rolls

1 pound fresh mushrooms,
  finely chopped
¼ cup butter
1 cup finely chopped Spam
1 (8-ounce) package cream
  cheese, softened

1 tablespoon minced parsley
1 loaf sandwich bread, crusts
  removed
1 stick butter, melted (for
  brushing on rolls)

Sauté mushrooms in butter. Remove from heat and combine
with Spam, cream cheese, and parsley. Roll bread slices with a
rolling pin, or flatten slices with your hands. Spread bread with
cream cheese mixture. Roll each slice like a jellyroll. Cut each
roll into 3 pieces and fasten with a toothpick. Place on baking
pans. Brush each roll with melted butter and place under broiler until brown. Makes about 60.

Hawai'i's Spam Cookbook

Hot Crab Dip Mary

A winner!

1 (8-ounce) package cream
  cheese, softened
1 (7½-ounce) can crabmeat
2 tablespoons milk
¼ teaspoon salt

2 tablespoons minced onion
½ teaspoon horseradish
Pepper to taste
1 (3½-ounce) can French fried
  onion rings

Mix ingredients except onion rings. Place in small oven-proof dish suitable for serving. Sprinkle with onion rings. Bake uncovered at 375° for 15 minutes until bubbly. Serve with crackers.

The Friends of 'Iolani Palace Cookbook

Aloha Dip

1 (8-ounce) package cream
  cheese, softened
1 cup crushed pineapple,
  drained

1 cup grated coconut
1½ teaspoons ground ginger
1 teaspoon lemon juice
½ cup chopped pecans

Mash cream cheese well. Add remaining ingredients, and stir well. Chill for several hours before serving. Serve with crackers.

Pupus from Paradise

Aloha, pronounced ah-LO-ha, is a Hawaiian greeting, but means so much more than hello and goodbye. Aloha is the way people treat each other, a way of life, and a state of mind. Known as the Aloha State, Hawai'i is a string of 137 islands encompassing a land area of 6,422.6 square miles in the Pacific Ocean about 2,400 miles from the west coast of the continental United States. Stretching from northwest to southeast, the major islands are: Ni'ihau (Nee-ee-how), Kaua'i (ka-Wah-ee), O'ahu (Oh-Wa-who), Moloka'i (mo-lo-Kah-ee), Lana'i (la-Nah-ee), Kaho'olawe (kaw-ho-oh-la-vay), Maui (Mow-ee, rhymes with Now-ee), and Hawai'i (ha-Wa-ee or ha-Va-ee).

Baked Fresh Basil Dip

I received this recipe as part of a recipe chain letter. It originally called for a jar of artichoke hearts, chopped. I was making a pūpū (Hawaiian word for appetizer) for a friend's bridal shower and realized I did not have a jar of artichoke hearts. Out to the garden I went, found a large amount of basil, and this recipe has been changed forever. Everyone at the party asked for the recipe, so here it is.

1 cup packed, chopped fresh
  basil (or 1 jar artichoke
  hearts, chopped)
½ cup grated Parmesan
  cheese
¾ cup mayonnaise
2 cloves fresh garlic, chopped

Salt and pepper to taste
Tabasco sauce to taste (don't be
  stingy!)
1 teaspoon Dijon mustard
½ cup slivered almonds
  (optional)

Combine all of the ingredients, except slivered almonds, by hand or by blender or food processor. Spread mixture in bottom of an 8- or 9-inch baking dish. Spread almonds over the top and bake in 350° oven for 20 minutes. Serve immediately with crackers or bagel chips.

Shaloha Cookbook

Avocado-Crab Dip

1 large avocado, diced
1 tablespoon fresh lemon
  juice
2 tablespoons grated onion
1 tablespoon Worcestershire
  sauce

4 ounces cream cheese,
  softened
½ cup sour cream
½ teaspoon salt
1 (7½-ounce) can crabmeat,
  drained and flaked

Use firm avocado to avoid a messy-looking dip and toss, rather than mix, with lemon juice, onion, and Worcestershire sauce. Blend the cream cheese, sour cream, and salt; stir in. Add crabmeat and fold carefully into the seasoned avocado. Serve with tortilla chips or crackers.

Pupus–An Island Tradition

Over-the-Top Spinach Dip

¼ cup bread crumbs
2 tablespoons butter, melted
1 cup grated Parmesan
   cheese, divided
1 (8-ounce) package light
   cream cheese, softened
8 ounces mozzarella cheese,
   shredded
1 (1-ounce) envelope Lipton
   Golden Onion Recipe Soup
   Mix

1 cup light sour cream
2 cloves garlic, minced
3 (6-ounce) jars marinated
   artichoke hearts, drained,
   coarsely chopped
1 (6-ounce) can shrimp,
   drained
2 cups chopped fresh spinach
   leaves

Preheat oven to 350°. In a small bowl, combine bread crumbs, butter, and ½ cup Parmesan cheese; set aside. Combine remaining ingredients; spoon into a 2-quart casserole dish. Cover; bake 25–30 minutes, until bubbly. Remove from oven; sprinkle with bread crumb mixture. Continue baking uncovered 5–7 minutes. Serves 12.

Dd's Table Talk II

After watching the sun rise so spectacularly over the top of Mt. Haleakala, Gwen and Barney didn't meet any other grandparents bike riding the 38 miles all the way down to the beach. (The key word here is "down.") The sheer exhilaration of having achieved this feat was only surpassed by the adventurous thrill of this never-to-be-forgotten ride.

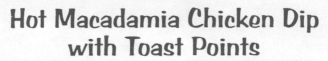

Hot Macadamia Chicken Dip with Toast Points

Crunchy roasted mac nuts top this creamy, flavorful chicken dip.

8 slices homemade-style
  wheat bread
1 (8-ounce) package light
  cream cheese, softened
2 tablespoons milk
1½ cups minced cooked
  chicken or turkey
2 teaspoons prepared
  horseradish

½ cup sour cream
¼ cup finely chopped green
  pepper
1 green onion, chopped
½ teaspoon garlic salt
¼ teaspoon cracked pepper
1 cup chopped macadamia nuts
  or pecans
2 teaspoons butter

Remove crusts from bread and cut each slice into 4 triangles. Toast bread on a baking sheet in preheated 400° oven until browned and very crisp, 5–7 minutes. Meanwhile, in a mixing bowl, beat cream cheese and milk until smooth with electric mixer or by hand. Stir in chicken, horseradish, sour cream, green pepper, onion, garlic salt, and pepper.

Spoon into an ungreased shallow 2-cup baking ramekin or crock. Set aside. In a skillet, sauté the nuts at medium heat in butter for 3–4 minutes, or until lightly browned. Sprinkle over cream cheese mixture. Bake, uncovered, at 350° for 20 minutes. Serve with toast points. Yields 32 or more pūpū servings.

Kona on My Plate

Haleakala, in Maui, is the world's largest dormant volcano with its last eruption thought to be sometime around 1790. The summit of Haleakala is 10,023 feet above sea level and is the highest point of Maui.

Fiery Pupu Wings

2½ pounds chicken wings,   Oil for frying
cut at joints (or drumettes)

MARINADE:

2 cloves garlic, minced
1 tablespoon sesame seed oil
1 tablespoon brown sugar
1 tablespoon soy sauce
1 tablespoon dry sherry
2 teaspoons sake (rice wine)

2 teaspoons fresh grated ginger
1 teaspoon cayenne pepper
1 teaspoon salt
Pinch freshly ground black
pepper and red pepper flakes

In a small bowl, combine chicken with Marinade ingredients. Marinate 2 hours.

BATTER:

½ cup flour
½ cup cornstarch

2 large eggs, beaten
¾ cup water

In a wok or deep fryer, heat oil. In a mixing bowl, combine Batter ingredients. Dip drained chicken into batter; deep-fry until golden.

SAUCE:

¼ soy sauce
2 tablespoons brown sugar
2 tablespoons rice wine vinegar
2 tablespoons sesame seed oil
2 cloves garlic, minced

2 teaspoons minced fresh
ginger
2 stalks green onions, chopped
1 teaspoon Thai chili garlic
paste

In a mixing bowl, combine Sauce ingredients. Drizzle over chicken. Serves 8.

Dd's Table Talk II

pūpū [poo-poo] – The Hawaiian term for any hot or cold appetizer, which can include a wide range of items such as macadamia nuts and won tons.

Coconut Chicken Bites

3½ cups sweetened, shredded
 coconut
2 teaspoons ground cumin
¾ teaspoon ground coriander
½ teaspoon cayenne pepper
Salt and freshly ground
 pepper

2 pounds boneless, skinless
 chicken breasts, cut into
 1-inch pieces
2 eggs, beaten
Dijon mustard for dipping

Preheat oven to 325°. Bake coconut on large, heavy baking sheet until golden brown, stirring frequently, about 15 minutes. Transfer to bowl and cool. Coarsely grind coconut in batches in food processor and place on large plate. Spray 2 large, heavy cookie sheets with cooking spray.

In a large bowl, combine cumin, coriander, cayenne, salt, and pepper. Dredge chicken pieces in seasonings, turning to coat. Dip into beaten eggs. Dredge chicken pieces in coconut, coating completely. Transfer to prepared cookie sheets. Cover and chill for one hour. (Can be prepared one day in advance.)

Preheat oven to 400°. Bake chicken until crisp and golden brown, about 15 minutes, turning pieces over once during baking. Arrange chicken on platter. Serve warm or at room temperature with Dijon mustard for dipping. Serves 6–8.

Kailua Cooks

Macadamia Chicken Strips

2 cups flour
1–2 teaspoons salt
  (depending on saltiness
  of nuts)
12 ounces roasted macadamia
  nuts, finely chopped

1 pound chicken, boned, cut in
  strips ³⁄₄x3 inches long
½ cup butter, melted
4 eggs, lightly beaten

Preheat oven to 350°. Pour flour and salt into a plastic bag. Place nuts into another plastic bag. Taking a small handful at a time, dip chicken strips in melted butter to coat, then put in flour-filled bag. Shake to coat; shake off excess flour. Dip in beaten eggs. Shake off excess egg and place in macadamia-nut-filled bag. Shake to coat. Place chicken strips on ungreased, nonstick cookie sheet, and bake 20 minutes. Store in refrigerator in an airtight container, if prepared ahead. Serve at room temperature.

Note: This can also be frozen. Thaw and serve at room temperature, or warm in oven before serving. Chopped pecans can be used in place of the macadamia nuts.

Pupus–An Island Tradition

Chicken Roll

2½ cups chopped, cooked
  chicken breasts
½ cup finely chopped celery
2 tablespoons chopped parsley
2 tablespoons chopped
  watercress

½ cup mayonnaise
1 teaspoon horseradish
Dash Tabasco
Macadamia nuts, chopped

Mix all ingredients, except nuts. Roll into 1-inch bar; roll in chopped nuts. Wrap in foil. Chill. Unwrap and slice to serve. Serve on party rye bread or crackers.

Pupus from Paradise

Stir-Fried Beef with Lettuce

4 medium shiitake (Japanese
 black) mushrooms
1 ¼ pounds ground beef
4 tablespoons peanut oil
2 slices ginger, finely minced
4 ounces bamboo shoots,
 coarsely minced
2 cloves garlic, finely minced
4 water chestnuts, coarsely
 minced
1 stalk scallion (green onion),
 chopped

1 teaspoon salt
¼ teaspoon pepper
1 tablespoon light shoyu
½ tablespoon black bean
 paste
½ tablespoon hoisin sauce
½ tablespoon sugar
1 tablespoon rice wine or dry
 sherry
1 ½ teaspoons sesame oil
2 sprigs parsley to garnish
12 lettuce leaves

Soak mushrooms in hot water for 30 minutes; remove and discard stems. Coarsely mince the caps. Fry beef until browned; drain fat.

In hot oil, stir-fry ginger and mushrooms for 30 seconds before adding bamboo shoots, garlic, and water chestnuts. After 1 minute, add scallions and meat together with the salt and pepper. Cook another 2 minutes, stirring constantly. Add the shoyu, bean paste, hoisin sauce, sugar, and rice wine, and cook another 3 minutes. Add sesame oil and serve garnished with sprigs of parsley. People will help themselves to a couple of spoonfuls of the minced mixture by placing it on a lettuce leaf, wrapping it up carefully, and eating it with their fingers.

Pupus–An Island Tradition

Hawai'i has its own time zone, Hawai'i-Aleutian Standard Time. Hawai'i does not observe Daylight Savings Time. Therefore, in the summer, the islands are three hours behind Pacific Standard Time, four hours behind Mountain Standard Time, etc. In the winter, they are four hours behind Pacific Daylight Savings Time, five hours behind Mountain Standard Time, and so on.

Teriyaki Meatballs

1½ pounds ground beef
2 tablespoons flour
2 eggs
1 teaspoon salt
Dash of pepper
2 tablespoons cornstarch

¼ cup sugar
⅓ cup shoyu
1 (14-ounce) can beef broth
¼ cup sake
2 tablespoons minced ginger
2 teaspoons minced garlic

Combine beef, flour, eggs, salt, and pepper. Mix lightly and shape into small balls. Place in greased baking pan and bake at 400° for 14–17 minutes. Mix cornstarch, sugar, shoyu, beef broth, sake, ginger, and garlic and cook until thick. Add meatballs and simmer. Makes about 50 meatballs.

Note: Mix lean and 25– to 30-percent fat ground beef equally for better flavor. The meatballs can be made ahead and frozen. Thaw and heat in the sauce and serve. Instant pūpū.

Pupus–An Island Tradition

Polynesian Meat Balls

1 egg
½ cup water
1 pound ground chuck or
ground turkey

1 (8-ounce) can water
chestnuts, drained, minced
½ cup seasoned bread crumbs

Combine egg and water and beat well. Add remaining ingredients, mixing lightly. Shape into balls and bake on foil-lined cookie sheet for 30 minutes at 350°. Serve in chafing dish with Sauce. Makes about 60–65 meat balls. Meat balls may be prepared in advance and frozen.

SAUCE:
⅔ cup apricot-pineapple
preserves
1 tablespoon prepared
horseradish
¼ cup soy sauce

1 clove garlic, minced, and/or
1 tablespoon minced onion
⅔ cup water
1 tablespoon lemon juice

Bring to a boil, stirring well. Add meat balls and let simmer slowly in Sauce.

Pupus from Paradise

Kailua Crab Cakes

1 pound fresh lump crabmeat
1½ cups panko flakes
2 eggs, well beaten
1 tablespoon Dijon mustard
½ teaspoon Worcestershire
 sauce

2 tablespoons minced parsley
¼ cup chopped scallions
1 teaspoon Old Bay Seasoning
½ cup mayonnaise
Panko flakes to coat
¼ cup cooking oil

Place crabmeat in mixing bowl with 1½ cups panko flakes. Add remaining ingredients, except panko to coat, and cooking oil. Mix gently, leaving the crab lumps as large as possible. Shape mixture into 12–16 equal portions; ball up and flatten into a patty shape about ¾ to 1 inch thick. Coat each crab cake with panko flakes. Chill for at least one hour before cooking.

 Heat cooking oil over medium heat. Sauté each cake for 2–2½ minutes per side in the oil. Makes approximately 12–16 petite cakes, or 4–5 dinner-size crab cakes.

TARTAR SAUCE FOR KAILUA CRAB CAKES:

2 tablespoons tarragon
 vinegar
1 teaspoon Dijon mustard
½ teaspoon kosher salt
Pinch cayenne pepper
⅓ cup finely chopped
 cornichons (gherkins)

1 tablespoon finely chopped
 shallots
1 teaspoon finely chopped
 capers
1 tablespoon finely chopped
 leaf parsley
1 cup mayonnaise

Combine ingredients and refrigerate until ready to serve. Makes 1½ cups.

Kailua Cooks

Does Hawai'i have seasons? Sure it does! There are two main seasons in Hawai'i. Summer, called Kau, extends from May to October and has an average daytime temperature of 85 degrees F. Winter, called Ho'oilo, runs from November to April with an average daytime temperature of 78 degrees F.

Lomi Salmon

1 pound salted salmon
3 large tomatoes, diced
1 onion, chopped

3 stalks green onions, chopped
3 cubes ice, cracked

Soak salted salmon in cold water for one hour. If salmon is very salty, repeat process. Remove skin and bones, and shred salmon with fingers. Place in a bowl and add tomatoes and onions. Chill; add crushed ice just before serving.

Note: Salted salmon was introduced to Hawaiians by Westerners. Lomi salmon is now known as a "traditional" Hawaiian food, which is always served at a lū'au.

Ethnic Foods of Hawai'i

The lei custom was introduced to the Hawaiian Islands by early Polynesian voyagers. These garlands, constructed mainly of flowers, leaves, shells, seeds, or feathers, were worn by ancient Hawaiians to beautify themselves. With the advent of tourism in the islands, the lei quickly became *the* symbol of Hawai'i to millions of visitors worldwide.

Pan Sushi

SUSHI RICE:

3 cups rice, cooked
½ cup Japanese rice vinegar

½ cup sugar
1 teaspoon salt

Put hot rice in a large bowl. In small bowl, mix together vinegar, sugar, and salt. Sprinkle half of the sauce on hot rice and mix with wooden spoon or rice paddle. Taste; add more sauce to taste.

Wet 9x13-inch pan. Shake off excess water and spread rice in the pan evenly. Place a piece of wax paper over rice and press down gently. Remove wax paper. Top rice with Shoyu Tuna and your choice of Toppings. Cool at least 30 minutes. Cut into squares with a wet knife. Makes 24 squares.

SHOYU TUNA:

1 (6-ounce) can tuna
2 tablespoons sugar

2 tablespoons shoyu

Drain tuna; place it in a small saucepan and add sugar and shoyu. Stir and cook 1–2 minutes. Sprinkle over Sushi Rice.

SUGGESTED TOPPINGS:

Colored shrimp flakes
Sliced takuwan
Pickled ginger

Thinly sliced veggies such as
  carrots and cucumbers
Thin slices of nori (seaweed)

Aunty Pua's Keiki Cookbook

Oriental Fresh Mushrooms

16 fresh mushrooms, 1–1½
  inches in diameter
Lemon juice
½ pound ground pork
¼ cup minced water
  chestnuts

¼ cup minced green onions
1 egg, slightly beaten
1 teaspoon soy sauce
¼ teaspoon garlic powder
¼ stick butter, melted
¼ cup untoasted sesame seeds

Preheat oven to 350°. Clean mushrooms; remove and reserve stems. If preparing in advance, rub with lemon juice. Chop mushroom stems finely and combine with pork, water chestnuts, green onions, egg, soy sauce, and garlic powder. Stuff caps with mixture and coat cap bottoms with butter. Top with sesame seeds. Put in large baking dish and bake for 30–40 minutes. Serve immediately.

Pupus–An Island Tradition

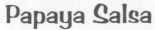

Papaya Salsa

This salsa is a refreshing complement to the smoky, salty flavor of grilled seafood.

3 cups diced ripe papaya
1 cup diced tomatoes
1 cup finely diced red bell pepper
1½ cups diced red onion
½ jalapeño pepper, seeded and finely chopped
2 tablespoons extra virgin olive oil
2½ tablespoons red wine vinegar

6 tablespoons freshly squeezed lime juice
2 tablespoons freshly squeezed lemon juice
2 teaspoons ground cumin
1 teaspoon freshly ground black pepper
Dash Tabasco
1 cup coarsely chopped, loosely packed Chinese parsley

Combine all ingredients in a large porcelain or glass bowl. Toss thoroughly. Cover and let stand for 1 or 2 hours. Serve chilled or at room temperature. Makes 1 quart.

Note: Salsa will keep in the refrigerator for up to a week.

Another Taste of Aloha

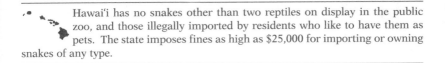

Hawai'i has no snakes other than two reptiles on display in the public zoo, and those illegally imported by residents who like to have them as pets. The state imposes fines as high as $25,000 for importing or owning snakes of any type.

Parsley and Coconut Sambol

This is a delicious and refreshing sambol that can be served as an appetizer (with crackers) or as an accompaniment to seafood and fish. It should be used within a day or two.

2 cups parsley leaves, washed
½ cup grated fresh coconut
2 green chiles, halved, seeded, and chopped
¼ teaspoon freshly ground black pepper

2 limes, juiced and strained
Salt to taste
½ teaspoon sugar

Place all ingredients in food processor and blend until smooth. Taste; adjust seasoning by adding more lime juice, salt, or sugar. Spoon into a glass bowl. Serve chilled. Makes 4 servings.

Burst of Flavor

Mango Salsa

1 large mango, peeled, pitted, and diced
3 tablespoons chopped onion
3 tablespoons chopped green bell pepper
3 tablespoons chopped red bell pepper
1 teaspoon minced fresh chives

1½ tablespoons white wine vinegar
1 tablespoon minced fresh cilantro
1 tablespoon olive oil
½ avocado, diced
Salt and pepper to taste

Mix all ingredients, except avocado, in large bowl. Right before serving, add avocado along with salt and pepper to taste and stir gently. Great with chips or on grilled chicken. Makes 2 cups.

Kailua Cooks

Hawaiian Fruit Kabobs

1 (14-ounce) can pineapple
  chunks, drained, reserve
  juice
1½ teaspoons finely chopped,
  fresh mint leaves

1 tablespoon lemon juice
1 large banana
1 large papaya
Maraschino cherries (optional)

Combine reserved pineapple juice, mint leaves, and lemon juice.
Cut peeled banana and papaya into 1-inch chunks. Marinate
fruit in juice for 5 or more minutes. Alternate fruit on cocktail
skewers. Serve chilled. Makes 18–24 kabobs.

Pupus from Paradise

Creamy Fruit Dip

1 (8-ounce) package cream
  cheese
1 (7-ounce) jar marshmallow
  crème

Fruit such as apples, bananas,
  strawberries, firm mangoes,
  pears, peaches, and seedless
  grapes

Soften cream cheese by leaving it at room temperature for 30
minutes, or unwrap, place in a bowl, and microwave on MEDIUM
for 3–4 minutes. Put the cream cheese and marshmallow crème
in the mixing bowl and stir until they are blended together.

Wash fruit; cut into wedges or chunks. Put a toothpick in
each piece of fruit or put several fruits on skewers. Arrange the
fruit on a platter and serve with the dip.

Aunty Pua's Keiki Cookbook

Honolulu International Airport is home to the first runway built completely offshore. The "reef runway," a runway built on an artificial island created on the fringing reef of O'ahu's southern (Kona) coast, was completed in
October 1977. It is also used as an alternate landing sight for space shuttles.

Mixed Fruit Chutney

1½ cups cider vinegar
2 cups light brown sugar
1 teaspoon ground cinnamon
1 teaspoon salt
2 cloves garlic, minced
2 small, hot red peppers,
  seeded and chopped
1 cup chopped seedless prunes

1 cup seedless dark raisins
2 cups cored and chopped tart
  green apples
1 cup peeled and chopped ripe
  tomatoes
1 cup chopped onion
1 tablespoon grated lemon peel

In a saucepan, put vinegar, sugar, cinnamon, salt, garlic, and peppers and bring to a boil; add all other ingredients. Reduce heat, cover, and continue to cook, stirring often until mixture reaches desired consistency, about 30–45 minutes. Pour into hot, sterilized jars and seal. Makes 6–8 jars.

Paradise Preserves

Peanut Dipping Sauce

Use sauce for lumpia, shrimp rolls, etc. Sauce can be prepared one week ahead, covered, and refrigerated.

⅓ cup unsalted dry roasted
  peanuts
½ cup hoisin sauce
⅓–½ cup water

2 tablespoons plum sauce
½–¾ teaspoon ground red
  pepper paste (sambal
  oelek)

Coarsely chop peanuts; place in bowl. Mix in hoisin sauce, ⅓ cup water, plum sauce, and red pepper paste. If sauce is too thick, stir in remaining water.

Favorite Island Cookery Book V

Bread and Breakfast

The Aloha Tower is a prominent feature of the beautiful downtown Honolulu skyline. Standing 10 stories, it was once the tallest building in Hawai'i. Each side has a large clock face and A-L-O-H-A large enough to see for some distance in any direction.

Pineapple Nut Bread

2 cups flour
1 tablespoon baking powder
½ teaspoon salt
¼ teaspoon nutmeg
½ cup vegetable oil
¾ cup sugar

2 eggs
⅔ cup milk
1 teaspoon vanilla
1 (8-ounce) can crushed
  pineapple, drained
½ cup chopped pecans

Preheat oven to 350°; lightly oil and flour one loaf pan. Sift flour, baking powder, salt, and nutmeg onto wax paper. In a large bowl, beat oil with sugar; add eggs, one at a time; mix well. Add dry ingredients alternately with milk. Stir in vanilla; add pineapple and pecans. Bake for 50 minutes. Cool completely before cutting. Makes one loaf.

Dd's Table Talk

Hawaiian Macadamia Nut Bread

¼ cup butter, softened
¾ cup light brown sugar
2 eggs, beaten
1¾ cups flour
2 teaspoons baking powder
¼ teaspoon baking soda

½ teaspoon salt
¾ cup chopped macadamia
  nuts
1 cup shredded fresh
  pineapple, with juice

Cream butter and sugar; beat in eggs. Combine flour, baking powder, baking soda, and salt. Stir in nuts. Stir ½ flour mixture into creamed mixture. Gently stir in pineapple and remaining flour mixture. Turn batter into greased 9x5x3-inch pan. Bake one hour in preheated 350° oven, or until it tests done.

Seasoned with Aloha Vol. 2

Sadie's Purloined Banana Bread

A renowned recipe from my mother, this was "borrowed" 45 years ago by the chef at old Kona Inn. However, her secret ingredient—mace—was missing in his version, and it suffered by comparison.

2 cups raw sugar	2½ cups flour
1 cup butter, softened	1 teaspoon salt
6 ripe bananas, mashed	2 teaspoons baking soda
4 eggs, well beaten	1 teaspoon mace
1 teaspoon vanilla	

Cream sugar and butter together. Stir in mashed bananas, eggs, and vanilla. Sift dry ingredients. Mix dry and wet ingredients together just until combined. Don't overmix. Pour into 2 greased and floured 8x4x3-inch loaf pans. Bake in 350° preheated oven for 50 minutes, or until center feels firm to the touch. Yields 2 loaves.

Variation: May include chopped dates, golden raisins, chopped nuts, or other goodies.

Kona on My Plate

With Diamond Head as a backdrop, an early morning buffet breakfast right on the Waikiki Beach before it livens up for the day could not be any more delightful. We sampled all the fruits, some of which we had to ask the waiter to identify. I ate the center of the prickly red rambutan before I was told you don't eat the seed—wasn't too bad, but the white part surrounding it was much tastier!

Mia's Pineapple Bran Muffins

1 cup bran	⅓ cup butter, softened
1 cup buttermilk	½ cup brown sugar
1 cup flour	1 large egg
1 teaspoon cinnamon	¼ cup molasses
1 teaspoon baking powder	¼ cup crushed pineapple
½ teaspoon baking soda	⅓ cup chopped dates or
½ teaspoon salt	raisins

Combine bran and buttermilk. Mix together flour, cinnamon, baking powder, baking soda, and salt. Add, all at once, to bran mix. Stir just until blended. Cream butter, sugar, egg, and molasses thoroughly. Blend into bran mixture. Stir in pineapple and dates. Put liners in 12 muffin tins. Fill each muffin cup ¾ full. Bake at 400° for 20–25 minutes. Cool slightly. Remove liners.

GLAZE:

½ cup honey	1 tablespoon butter
2 tablespoons corn syrup	

Melt honey, corn syrup, and butter in saucepan. Simmer 5 minutes. Dip muffin tops in Glaze, coating thoroughly. Place on a cookie sheet until Glaze is set. Serve warm. Makes 12 muffins.

Hawaii–Cooking with Aloha

The origin of the ukulele can be traced to immigrant Manual Nunes who arrived in Hawai'i from Madeira in 1879 to work in the sugar cane fields. He is responsible for transforming the Portuguese braguinha into the Hawaiian ukulele. Nunes established one of the first ukulele manufacturing companies and remained in business for over 40 years. The ukulele remains Hawai'i's most popular musical instrument.

Pineapple Corn Muffins

I have often enjoyed a cup of steaming Kona coffee with a muffin at various outdoor terraces along Waikiki. There always seems to be a wide choice of types of muffins with Hawaiian Island jams. Muffins are a legacy of missionary kitchens, but have been improved with Hawaiian flavors. This combination with pineapple and cornmeal is one of the best.

1 cup flour
¼ cup sugar
3 teaspoons baking powder
1 teaspoon salt
1 cup cornmeal or bran
¼ cup shortening or butter,
   softened

1 egg, beaten
½ cup milk
1 cup drained, crushed
   pineapple (canned or fresh)

Sift flour, sugar, baking powder, and salt together. Stir in cornmeal or bran. Blend in shortening with a fork or your fingertips to make a crumbly mixture. Add egg, milk, and pineapple, and stir to blend. Place in well-greased muffin pans. Bake at 425° for 15–20 minutes until golden brown. This will make about 2 dozen muffins.

Honolulu Hawaii Cooking

Mea 'Ono Paniolo
(Cowboy Coffeecake)

2⅓ cups sifted enriched flour	½ teaspoon cinnamon
½ teaspoon salt	½ teaspoon nutmeg
2 cups raw brown sugar	1 cup buttermilk
⅔ cup shortening	2 eggs, well beaten
2 teaspoons baking powder	½ cup chopped macadamia
½ teaspoon baking soda	nuts

Combine flour, salt, sugar, and shortening. Mix until crumbly. Reserve ½ cup of the mixture. To remaining crumbs, add baking powder, baking soda, and spices. Mix thoroughly. Add milk and eggs. Mix well. Pour into 2 wax-paper-lined, 8x8x2-inch baking pans. Sprinkle with reserved crumbs. Sprinkle chopped nuts and additional cinnamon on top. Bake at 375° for 25–30 minutes.

The Friends of 'Iolani Palace Cookbook

At 4,038 square miles, the island of Hawai'i is the state's largest single island, and is still growing. Located over a geologic hot spot, lava escapes to the surface and hardens, constantly expanding the island's size. Referred to as the Big Island, it is twice the size of all the other Hawaiian Islands combined.

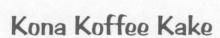

Kona Koffee Kake

1 cup brown or raw sugar
½ cup grated coconut
1 (8½-ounce) can crushed
   pineapple, drained,
   reserve juice
1½ cups flour

3 teaspoons baking powder
¾ teaspoon salt
¼ cup shortening
¾ cup juice-milk mix
   (reserved pineapple juice)
2 eggs

Preheat oven to 375°. Grease a round 9x1½-inch pan or a square 8x8x2-inch pan. Blend the sugar, coconut, and pineapple in a mixing bowl. Reserve ½ cup of this mixture. Add the remaining ingredients to the mix in the bowl and beat vigorously one minute. Pour batter evenly into prepared pan. Bake about 30 minutes or until a toothpick inserted into the center comes out clean. Remove cake from pan and place on serving dish. Spread reserved sugar mix over top of cake. Serve cake warm with butter or margarine and, of course, coffee.

Kau Kau Kitchen

Hiroko's Breakfast Biscuit

4 cups flour
½ cup sugar
1 teaspoon baking powder
1 teaspoon baking soda
1 stick butter

1 stick margarine
1½ cups or less milk
1 teaspoon vanilla
¼ cup sugar mixed with ½–1
   teaspoon cinnamon

Combine dry ingredients in large bowl. Add butter and margarine and cut in till pea-size. Add milk and vanilla to form dough. Roll out and cut into long thin strips; spiral from one end (like a snail) to form biscuit. Sprinkle with cinnamon sugar. Bake 25–30 minutes at 375°. Serve when golden brown.

A Lei of Recipes

Coffee Jelly

½ package unflavored gelatin   3 cups black coffee
½ cup cold water   ¾ cup sugar

Soak gelatin in cold water and dissolve in the hot coffee. Add sugar and stir until it dissolves. Strain and turn into a mold. Serve with whipped cream.

How to Use Hawaiian Fruit

Papaya Jelly

½ package unflavored gelatin   1 cup boiling water
½ cup cold water   1 cup papaya pulp
½ cup sugar   Juice of 1 lemon

Soak gelatin in cold water 5 minutes. Dissolve sugar in boiling water; add gelatin and strain. When cool, add papaya and lemon juice. Place on ice (refrigerate) to harden.

How to Use Hawaiian Fruit

Winds move from east to west across the islands of Hawai'i, and as a result, the volcanic mountains trap the moist air from the Pacific on the windward sides (east and north). This phenomenon results in a cool, wet windward side, and a warm, dry leeward side (west and south). For example, on the windward side of Maui, the top of the West Maui Mountain receives over 400 inches of rainfall per year, and on the leeward side, the city of Kihei receives less than 10 inches of rain per year.

Nutty Garlic Loaf

1 (1-pound) package frozen
bread dough
2 tablespoons butter, melted
2 tablespoons chopped salted
peanuts or macadamia nuts

3 garlic cloves, minced
1 tablespoon freeze-dried
chives
1 tablespoon Parmesan cheese

Let bread dough thaw at room temperature until it can be cut with a knife. Slice into 10 equal slices.

Mix butter, nuts, garlic, and chives. Dip bread slices into this mixture. Put slices upright in an 8½x4½x2½-inch lightly greased bread pan. Drizzle any remaining butter mixture over top of loaf. Sprinkle with Parmesan cheese. Let dough rise in warm place until loaf reaches top of pan. Bake at 375° for 25–30 minutes or until loaf is golden brown. Makes 10 slices.

Hilo Woman's Club Cookbook

Garlic Bread Plus

You won't know what hit you when you bite into this delectable garlic bread—it tastes at once buttery, cheesy, and indescribably rich—and it is.

1 baguette (long French bread)
1½ tablespoons butter,
softened
2 large cloves garlic, pressed
½ cup of your favorite
mayonnaise

¼ cup grated mozzarella
cheese
⅓ cup Parmesan cheese
1 tablespoon minced fresh
herbs (optional)
¼ teaspoon salt (optional)

Preheat broiler, and set baking rack about 4 inches beneath heat source.

Split bread in half lengthwise. Combine remaining ingredients and mix them well. Slather the cut surfaces of bread with mayonnaise mixture, and place on baking tray or cookie sheet in broiler. Broil until bubbly and lightly browned. Cut into pieces and serve immediately. Yields about 10 pieces.

Vegetarian Nights

Skillet Corn Fritters

These are a delicious accompaniment to fish, meat, or poultry dishes, or can be eaten as a snack.

¼ cup skim milk	Dash salt
½ cup unbleached flour	Dash black pepper
1 (10-ounce) package frozen corn kernels, thawed	2 egg whites
3 tablespoons chopped fresh parsley	

In a large bowl stir skim milk into flour until blended well. Stir in corn, parsley, salt, and pepper. In another bowl beat egg whites until stiff peaks form. Fold the beaten egg whites gently into corn mixture, making sure to mix thoroughly. Spray skillet with cooking spray and heat on medium heat. Drop mixture by tablespoonfuls onto pan, leaving space between them. Cook for about 2 minutes, or until browned slightly; turn and cook other side for about 2 minutes more. Makes about 8 fritters.

Note: To reheat, place on a paper towel, and put in the microwave for about 10 seconds each.

Nutritional analysis per serving: Cal 66; Fat .59mg; Chol 0mg; Sod 50mg

The Best of Heart-y Cooking

Soups and Salads

The world-famous Polynesian Cultural Center in O'ahu showcases seven South Pacific island cultures in each of their villages. Events include a lū'au, Pageant of the Long Canoes, IMAX™ Theater, and "Horizons" evening show.

Kim Chee Soup with Meat and Tofu

This is a spicy soup, often eaten when one feels like he is coming down with a cold.

1 pound sliced pork, bite-sized, or 1–2 cans Spam, cubed
⅛ cup sesame oil, divided
3–4 cups kim chee, with liquid
1 bag soy bean sprouts
Water
1 wooden spoonful of ko choo jung
¼ cup soy sauce, or to taste
Salt and pepper to taste
1 (12-ounce) block firm tofu, cubed

Brown meat in a little sesame oil on medium-high heat. Drain fat; add kim chee, soy bean sprouts, just enough water to cover, ko choo jung, remaining sesame oil, soy sauce, and salt and pepper to taste. Heat to boiling, then reduce to simmer for about 15 minutes, stirring occasionally. Add tofu and simmer for 15–30 more minutes until kim chee is cooked.

West Kauai's Plantation Heritage

Mahi Chowder

4 slices bacon, diced
1 cup diced onion
6 cups water, divided
1 bay leaf, wrinkled
3 potatoes, diced
2 pounds mahi, cubed
2 cups powdered milk, dry
Salt
White pepper

Fry bacon and onion in the bottom of your soup pot until the onion is browned. Add 4 cups water, the bay leaf, and potatoes. Bring water up to boiling and let it simmer until the potatoes are tender. Add mahi. Mix dry milk with remaining water and add it to the pot. When the mahi is tender, add salt and white pepper to taste, and serve. You may want to serve this with a crispy green salad and crusty brown bread.

Kau Kau Kitchen

Portuguese Bean Soup

1 pound pinto beans
2½ quarts water
1 ham bone
½ pound bacon
2 stalks celery, chopped
2 medium onions, chopped
2 tablespoons flour
Small bunch parsley, chopped
2 bay leaves
1 pound precooked carrots, chopped

2 teaspoons chopped garlic
½ teaspoon ground pepper
2 teaspoons seasoning salt
½ cup sherry
2 Portuguese sausages, chopped
½ cup cubed ham
½ head cabbage, chopped
3 potatoes, precooked and cubed
Dash cinnamon

Wash beans and soak overnight in cold water. Drain and rinse. Place in stockpot with 2½ quarts water and ham bone. Cover and simmer. While beans simmer, cook bacon, remove, and cut into small pieces. To the bacon grease, add celery and onions, and sauté until onion is translucent. Add flour and stir one minute. Add this mixture to stockpot with remaining ingredients. Mix thoroughly. Simmer over low heat for at least 4 hours.

Tailgate Party Cookbook

Nine Bean Soup

2 cups Bean Soup Mix
2 quarts warm water
1 pound lean ham, diced
1 large onion, chopped
1 clove garlic, minced

½ teaspoon salt (optional)
1 (28-ounce) can tomatoes,
    undrained and chopped
1 (4-ounce) can diced chiles

Sort and wash bean mix. Place in Dutch oven. Cover beans with water level 2 inches above beans. Soak overnight.

Drain beans. Add 2 quarts water and next 4 ingredients. Cover and bring to a boil, reduce heat, and simmer 1½ hours or until beans are tender. Add remaining ingredients and simmer for 30 minutes, stirring occasionally. Yields 8 cups.

Variation: Use Portuguese sausage, ham hock, or a mix of sausage, bacon, and ham.

BEAN SOUP MIX:
1 pound barley pearls
1 pound dried pink beans
1 pound dried red beans
1 pound dried pinto beans
1 pound dried navy beans
    or small white beans

1 pound dried Great Northern
    beans
1 pound dried lentils
1 pound dried split peas
    (yellow or green)
1 pound dried black-eyed peas

Combine all beans. Divide into 10 (2-cup) packages for gift giving. Enclose the above Nine Bean Soup recipe.

Variations: Any combination of beans or use kidney, black, or lima beans.

Favorite Recipes for Islanders

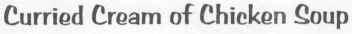

Curried Cream of Chicken Soup

2 tablespoons butter
3 tablespoons flour
Dash of pepper
3 cups chicken broth
1 cup 2% milk
1½ cups chopped, cooked
chicken

½ cup shredded cheese (or
more)
Poultry seasoning
Curry powder
Salt and pepper to taste

In a large saucepan, melt butter, then stir in flour and a dash of pepper. Add chicken broth and milk. Cook and stir until bubbly. Cook and stir one minute more. Stir in the chicken; heat through. Add cheese until soup is at your desired consistency and flavor, then add poultry seasoning, curry powder, salt and pepper to taste. Yields 3 main-dish servings.

Seasoned with Aloha Vol. 2

Velvet Corn Soup with Crab

¼ pound ground pork
1 teaspoon minced fresh
ginger
1 tablespoon vegetable oil
10 cups chicken stock
2 tablespoons sherry
12 ounces creamed corn
3 tablespoons cornstarch
dissolved in 4 tablespoons
water

3 egg whites, slightly beaten
10 ounces fresh or frozen crab,
flaked
Salt and pepper to taste
4 green onions, thinly sliced for
garnish

In a large saucepan, sauté ground pork and ginger in oil. Add stock, sherry, and corn, and bring to a boil. Thicken with cornstarch-water mixture. Slowly stir in egg whites. Add crab and season. Remove from heat. Garnish and serve. Serves 10.

A Taste of Aloha

Chilled Avocado Cream Soup

1 large ripe avocado
1½ cups chicken broth
1½ tablespoons fresh lime
  juice
1 teaspoon salt

¼ teaspoon pepper
½ teaspoon chile pepper
  water or dash of Tabasco
½ cup whipping cream

Peel, stone, and dice the avocado. Put all ingredients except cream into a blender in order given, and blend until smooth. Check seasoning. Add more to taste. Chill covered, and before serving, stir in cream.

Joys of Hawaiian Cooking

Red Bell Pepper and Potato Cream Soup

4 red bell peppers, seeded
  and cut into thin strips
1 potato, peeled and cut into
  very thin strips
1 large onion, cut into thin
  strips
3–4 fresh garlic cloves,
  peeled and cut thinly

2 tablespoons butter
Sweet Hungarian paprika
Freshly ground black pepper
Oregano
Chicken broth (about 2 cups)

Sauté peppers, potato, onion, and garlic in butter, until soft and translucent. Add seasonings to taste. Pour into food processor and process until smooth. Heat and thin to desired consistency with chicken broth.

Tropical Taste

Ellen's Favorite Cioppino
(Fish Stew)

¼ cup olive oil
2 large onions, chopped
2 green peppers, seeded and chopped
6 celery stalks, chopped
5 cloves garlic, pressed or minced
1 cup minced parsley, divided
1 (48-ounce) can V-8 juice
1½ cups dry red wine
1½ cups dry white wine
1 (8-ounce) bottle clam juice
1 (6-ounce) can tomato paste

3 teaspoons dried oregano
3 teaspoons dried basil
4 bay leaves
1 teaspoon crushed red pepper flakes
2 teaspoons sugar
Salt and pepper to taste
3 pounds fish fillets, cut into 1-inch chunks
1 pound shrimp, peeled and deveined
2 pounds other seafood (crabs, scallops, clams)

Heat olive oil in a heavy pot over medium-high heat. Add onions, peppers, celery, garlic, and ¾ of the parsley, and sauté until vegetables are soft (do not overcook). Add all other ingredients except the seafood; stir until well blended and bring to just below the boiling point. Reduce heat and simmer stock for ½ hour. Stir frequently.

Add the seafood in order given: fish, shrimp, crabs, scallops, and clams last. Cook only until seafood is done, approximately 10–15 minutes. Serve in bowls topped with remaining parsley. Serves 6.

Note: The stock can be made ahead of time and frozen with only the seafood to be added at a later date.

Fresh Catch of the Day...from the Fishwife

Eighteen television series have been filmed in Hawai'i since 1968, some of which include: *Hawaii Five-O, Fantasy Island, Magnum P.I., Tour of Duty, Jake and the Fatman, Raven, The Byrds of Paradise,* and *Baywatch Hawaii.*

Seared Sesame 'Ahi Salad

SAUCE:

8 ounces shiitake mushrooms, julienned
¼ cup sliced garlic
1 cup cubed tomatoes
½ cup sesame seed oil, divided

¼ cup lemon juice
¼ cup chopped cilantro
½ cup soy sauce
½ cup olive oil

Sauté shiitake mushrooms with garlic and tomatoes in ¼ cup sesame seed oil. In a bowl, add lemon juice, cilantro, soy sauce, and remaining oils. Combine mushrooms, garlic, and tomatoes with lemon juice-cilantro-soy sauce mixture.

4 (4-ounce) pieces (1-pound) 'ahi
1 cup sesame seeds
½ cup olive oil
¼ cup balsamic vinegar
½ pound baby mixed greens

12 Belgian endive leaves
Salt and pepper to taste
Sauce
2 whole Roma tomatoes
½ cup chopped macadamia nuts

Roll the 'ahi in sesame seeds and sear it very quickly (in hot oiled skillet). Mix olive oil and balsamic vinegar together for vinaigrette. Mix baby salad greens with vinaigrette. Place Belgian endive on plate. Place baby mixed greens on endive. Slice the 'ahi and arrange on top of the greens. Top 'ahi with Sauce and garnish with tomato fans and macadamia nuts. Makes 4 servings.

Friends and Celebrities Cookbook II

Chinese-Style Chicken Salad

Chicken salad is everyone's favorite. It is adaptable and can be served on dozens of occasions. It can be dressed down and taken on a picnic or dressed up and served at a dinner party.

1 medium head lettuce,
  shredded
½ cup minced green onions
1 bunch Chinese parsley
  (cilantro), chopped
¼ cup thinly sliced celery
  (optional)
1 (3-ounce) package fried
  won ton strips

¼ cup chopped, roasted
  peanuts
1 pound cooked, boneless
  chicken breasts, shredded
½ cup char siu (roast
  barbecued pork), julienned

Combine lettuce, onions, Chinese parsley, and celery in a large salad bowl; toss to mix well. Sprinkle with won ton strips, peanuts, chicken, and char siu.

SESAME VINEGAR DRESSING:
2 tablespoons toasted sesame
  seeds
1 teaspoon salt
½ teaspoon pepper

¼ cup sugar
⅓ cup rice vinegar
¼ cup salad oil

Combine ingredients; mix well, and pour over salad just before serving. Serves 6–10.

Variation: For Chinese Crab Salad, substitute 1 cup cooked crabmeat for chicken.

The Tastes and Tales of Moiliili

Curried Chicken Salad in Tomato Petals

2 cups cooked and diced
  chicken
1 apple, pared and diced
½ cup diced celery
2 teaspoons grated onion
½ cup halved seedless grapes
⅓ cup toasted, slivered
  almonds

2 teaspoons curry powder
1 cup mayonnaise
1 teaspoon salt
Dash of pepper
6 tomatoes

Combine chicken, apple, celery, onion, grapes, and almonds. Blend curry powder with mayonnaise and seasonings; stir into chicken mixture. Chill. Cut tomatoes in sixths, almost but not all the way through, to form petals. Fill with chicken salad. Yields 6 servings.

Favorite Island Cookery Book II

Chinese Salad

½ pound chicken strips,
  cooked (or ham strips)
1 head lettuce, sliced thin
½ cup chopped green onions
½ cup thinly sliced celery

1 cup oil for frying
⅓ cup or 2 ounces mai fun
  (rice sticks)
12 won ton wrappers

Combine cooked chicken, lettuce, green onions, and celery in a bowl. Heat oil and deep-fry a handful of mai fun at a time until it rises to top of oil. Drain. Cut won ton wrappers into ¼-inch strips and deep-fry until brown; drain. Add mai fun and won ton strips to vegetables. Yields 6–8 servings.

SALAD DRESSING:

2 tablespoons oil
1 teaspoon salt
½ teaspoon pepper

6 tablespoons sugar
6 tablespoons vinegar
2 teaspoons oyster sauce

Combine all ingredients. Just before serving salad, toss with vegetables and chicken.

A Lei of Recipes

Turkey Salad

3 cups diced, cooked turkey
1 can water chestnuts,
  drained
½ cup chopped celery
¾ cup macadamia nuts
2 tablespoons vinegar

2 tablespoons crystallized
  ginger
¾ cup mayonnaise
1 teaspoon curry powder
1 tablespoon soy sauce
1½ cups diced pineapple

Combine turkey, water chestnuts, celery, and nuts. Add vinegar. Mix well. Add ginger. Combine mayonnaise, curry powder, soy sauce, and pineapple. Add to turkey mixture. Mix thoroughly. Chill several hours. Serve on lettuce or in hollowed out pineapple shell. Makes 8 servings.

Hawaii–Cooking with Aloha

Spam Pasta Salad

1 (12-ounce) bag pasta
  (veggie spirals are nice)
¼ medium onion, minced
1 cup diced Spam
1 (6-ounce) jar artichoke
  hearts, including juice
1 cup chopped cucumber or
  zucchini

⅓ cup Italian dressing
  (such as zesty Italian)
½ teaspoon salt
¼ teaspoon pepper
¼ teaspoon oregano
Sliced tomatoes, sliced hard-
  boiled eggs, olives, etc., for
  garnish

Cook pasta according to package directions. Do not overcook. Rinse with cold water and drain well.

Place all other ingredients in a bowl and mix together. Add drained pasta and toss together. Chill. Decorate top with sliced tomatoes, sliced hard-boiled eggs, olives, etc.

Hawai'i's Spam Cookbook

 Queen Lili'uokalani, the last reigning Hawaiian monarch, is best known to the world as the composer of many beautiful songs, including "Aloha Oe."

Honolulu Symphony Sweet Potato Salad

Great potluck offering for picnics, as flavors develop at air temperature.

CILANTRO LIME DRESSING:

1 teaspoon Dijon mustard	3 tablespoons oil
2 tablespoons fresh lime juice	½ teaspoon salt
3 tablespoons chopped fresh cilantro	¼ teaspoon ground black pepper
1 clove garlic, minced	

In a large bowl, whisk together mustard, lime juice, cilantro, and garlic. Slowly stream oil into bowl, whisking constantly. Stir in salt and black pepper.

2 large sweet potatoes, cooked, peeled, and cubed	1 cup corn kernels
1 cucumber, peeled, halved lengthwise, and sliced	½ red onion, thinly sliced
	¼ cup finely chopped peanuts

Add cool cubed sweet potatoes to dressing along with cucumber, corn, and red onion. Toss well. Serve at room temperature or chilled. Stir in the peanuts just before serving. Serves 6.

Kona on My Plate

 What's the weather like in Hawai'i? Sunny and warm, of course! Hawai'i is known for its perfect weather conditions—sunny and highs in the mid-80s with cool trade winds. Afternoon rain showers are not uncommon in the mountains and valleys on the northeastern side of the islands.

Macadamia Nut Pea Salad

DRESSING:

1½ teaspoons lemon juice
½ cup red wine vinegar
1 teaspoon salt
½ teaspoon freshly ground
  pepper
1½ teaspoons Worcestershire
  sauce

½ teaspoon Dijon mustard
1 clove garlic, crushed
2 tablespoons sugar
1½ teaspoons grated onion
  and juice
1½ cups corn oil

Blend all ingredients except the oil. Add oil and beat thoroughly. Store in the refrigerator if not used immediately.

1 (16-ounce) package frozen
  peas
1 cup chopped celery
¼ cup chopped green onions,
  including 3–4 inches of
  green tops
1 cup chopped macadamia
  nuts or cashews

¼ cup fried crisp and
  crumbled bacon
1 cup sour cream
½ teaspoon salt
¼ cup Dressing
Boston or Mānoa lettuce leaves

Turn frozen peas into a colander and rinse until thawed. Drain. Combine peas, celery, onions, nuts, and bacon. Mix sour cream, salt, and ¼ cup Dressing and pour over salad, mixing lightly. Cover and chill, preferably overnight. Serve on a bed of lettuce. Remaining Dressing may be refrigerated for later use.

Note: Onion juice is obtained by grating a large white onion on the fine side of a grater, or processing it in an electric blender and straining the purée. Serves 6.

Another Taste of Aloha

Mandarin Spinach Salad

This wonderful light spinach salad with oranges mixes up fast for a quick lunch or light supper. The Tarragon Dressing is completely nonfat, and can be made ahead and stored in a jar in the refrigerator.

4 cups fresh spinach, washed, dried, and torn
1 cup sliced fresh mushrooms
1 large tomato, cut into bite-size pieces
1 cup bean sprouts

1 (11-ounce) can Mandarin oranges (drain and reserve liquid)
1 tablespoon imitation bacon bits
Croutons (optional)

Combine all ingredients except oranges and bacon bits, and toss. Add oranges and bacon bits. Just before serving, pour dressing over salad and toss to coat well. Makes 4 servings. Add croutons, if desired.

TARRAGON DRESSING:
Reserved orange liquid
1 tablespoon raspberry wine vinegar
1 tablespoon white wine vinegar

2 teaspoons sugar
½ teaspoon ground white pepper
¼ teaspoon crushed tarragon leaves

Combine orange liquid, vinegars, sugar, pepper, and tarragon leaves. Shake well to combine.

Nutritional analysis per serving: Cal 150; Fat 1g; Chol 0mg; Sod 50mg

The Best of Heart-y Cooking

Christmas Salad Supreme

This beautiful salad draws rave reviews.

JAM VINAIGRETTE:

2 tablespoons raspberry or
  apple cider vinegar
⅓ cup vegetable oil

2 tablespoons raspberry or
  other fruit jam

Whisk all ingredients together. Place in small jar and refrigerate. Shake well before using.

SALAD:

¾ pound fresh spinach, torn
1 cup fresh or frozen
  raspberries, divided
10 fresh strawberries, halved

3 large kiwi, peeled and sliced
  thin, divided
¾ cup halved chopped
  pecans (or macadamia nuts)

Combine spinach, about ¾ of the berries, and two kiwi about one hour before serving. Drizzle with Jam Vinaigrette. Toss salad. Place in container with a tight lid. Chill, turning once. (If you use frozen berries, add them just before serving, or they will be too limp).

Just before serving, toss again with rest of berries and pecans, and garnish with last sliced kiwi.

Friends and Celebrities Cookbook II

Papaya Seed Salad Dressing

1 cup sugar	½ cup oil
1 teaspoon salt	1 small onion, chopped
½ teaspoon dry mustard	3 tablespoons papaya seeds
1 cup vinegar	

Combine ingredients and put in blender until papaya seeds are ground fine. Serve on fresh greens.

A Lei of Recipes

Special Salad Dressing

1 clove garlic, mashed	2 teaspoons salt
1 cup oil	½ teaspoon pepper
½ cup sugar	¼ cup mayonnaise
½ cup rice vinegar	1 teaspoon dry mustard

Mix ingredients in blender and chill. This dressing is delicious with fresh or cooked vegetables.

Variation: It may be used as marinade for fresh shrimp. Wash shrimp, remove legs, and soak with shell on in dressing overnight. Grill over coals.

Favorite Island Cookery Book VI

 Born and raised in Waikiki, Duke Kahanamoku, who is also known as the "Father of Modern Surfing," was a three-time Olympic Gold Medalist. Duke won his first Olympic gold medal and set a world record in the 100-meter free-style.

Fiesta Papaya Boats

2 papayas
2 cups shredded, cooked
  chicken
1 green onion, sliced
1 teaspoon sugar

¼ cup mayonnaise
1 cup grated, raw carrot
1 tablespoon wine vinegar
Salt and pepper to taste

Cut papayas in half and scoop out seeds. Combine all remaining ingredients, then spoon into cavities of papaya. Chill. Serves 4.

Hilo Woman's Club Cookbook

Herbed Carrot Slices

4 pounds carrots, peeled
  and thinly sliced
1 teaspoon salt
2⅔ cups white vinegar
2⅔ cups water
3 teaspoons dill seed
1 teaspoon mustard seed

1 teaspoon caraway seeds
1 teaspoon celery seeds
2 cups white sugar
2 teaspoons rock salt
1 teaspoon crushed and seeded
  Hawaiian chili pepper

Cook carrot slices with 1 teaspoon salt in very small amount of water until almost tender. Drain and pack the slices into hot sterilized jars and pour over them the hot syrup made by combining all the remaining ingredients in a pan, bringing to a full rolling boil, and boiling for 2 minutes. When syrup has covered carrots in the jars, seal them and let ripen for several weeks before serving.

Paradise Preserves

Polynesian Salad

1½ cups mayonnaise
1 cup mango chutney
2 pounds cooked, diced
  chicken
1 cup salted peanuts
  or macadamia nuts
1 cup golden raisins
1 cup flaked coconut

2 cups diagonally sliced
  bananas
Shredded lettuce
Avocado slices for garnish
Additional sliced banana for
  garnish
Lemon juice

Mix together mayonnaise and chutney; toss with chicken, nuts, and raisins. Gently combine with coconut and sliced bananas. Mound in a large bowl lined with shredded lettuce. Garnish with slices of avocado and banana dipped in lemon juice. Serves 10–12.

Hilo Woman's Club Cookbook

Dell Neely's Pineapple Pickles

6 cups fresh pineapple chunks
2 cups white sugar
1 cup cider vinegar

12 whole cloves
6 (2-inch) pieces cinnamon
  sticks

Put all ingredients into saucepan, bring to a boil, turn heat to medium, and continue cooking until pineapple turns a clear golden yellow. Pour fruit and syrup into hot, sterilized glass jars and seal. Let jars "ripen" about 2 weeks so fruit will absorb spices.

Paradise Preserves

Vegetables

Created by pounding taro root, poi is a staple in the Hawaiian diet and a traditional lū'au food. Poi, usually eaten with your fingers, is named based on the number of fingers needed to eat it: three-finger, two-finger, or the thickest, one-finger poi.

Tropical Sweet Potato Crunch

TOPPING:

⅓ cup firmly packed brown
  sugar
⅓ cup chopped macadamia
  nuts

⅓ cup shredded coconut
½ cup dried cranberries
2 tablespoons butter, melted

Preheat oven to 350°; lightly grease a 6-quart baking dish. In a small bowl; combine Topping ingredients; set aside.

4 pounds sweet potatoes,
  steamed, sliced
¼ cup brown sugar
½ cup pineapple juice
½ cup crushed pineapple
1 large egg, beaten
2 tablespoons butter, melted

½ teaspoon salt
½ teaspoon cinnamon
½ teaspoon ground cumin
1½ teaspoons vanilla extract
1 (16-ounce) can whole
  cranberry sauce

In a mixing bowl; combine potatoes with remaining ingredients, except cranberry sauce. Spoon half of potatoes into prepared dish. Spoon cranberry sauce over potatoes. Top with remaining potatoes and Topping mixture. Bake 30–35 minutes. Serves 10–12.

Variation: Optional to mash potatoes.

Dd's Table Talk II

Perfect Baked Sweet Potatoes

4 medium sweet potatoes   Safflower oil

Preheat oven to 400°. Wash and scrub potatoes; dry thoroughly. Coat potatoes lightly with oil. Prick surface with fork. Bake until tender, about 40–60 minutes.

Note: Rubbing potatoes with oil before baking makes them so creamy, they do not need additional butter. Makes 4 servings.

Favorite Island Cookery Book V

'Ono Sweet Potatoes

An old favorite with a tropical taste.

1 (24-ounce) can sweet potatoes or yams, drained	Brown sugar
3 ripe bananas	¼ cup macadamia nuts bits
1 teaspoon cinnamon	¼ cup crushed cornflakes
½ teaspoon salt	¼ cup butter, melted

Preheat oven to 350°. Mash sweet potatoes and bananas with cinnamon and salt. Place in a baking dish. Top with a thin layer of brown sugar. Mix nuts and cornflakes. Spread over brown sugar. Pour melted butter over top. Bake for 45–50 minutes. Serves 4–6.

A Taste of Aloha

Sweet Potato Tempura

Sweet potatoes	1 cup brown sugar
1 box mochiko (about 2 cups)	2½ cups water
1 cup flour	Oil for frying
½ teaspoon salt	

Cut sweet potatoes in shoe-string pieces. Rinse and drain in colander. Stir together mochiko, flour, salt, and brown sugar. Add water. Toss shoe-string potatoes in batter and deep-fry in hot oil. Drain on paper towels.

Favorite Recipes for Islanders

Kahoʻolawe, an uninhabited island less than 11 miles long, was taken over by the United States Navy at the beginning of World War II for use in bombing target practice. In the 1970s native Hawaiians began campaigning to regain the island from the U.S. Navy, and in 1994 the island was turned back over to the state of Hawaii. The state banned commercial activities, and efforts are underway to replant native vegetation and restore important historic sites.

Baked Stuffed Eggplant Parmigiano

Salt
1 large eggplant, peeled and
  sliced lengthwise ¼ inch
  thick (put 2 slices aside)
Egg wash (one beaten egg)
½ cup flavored bread crumbs
⅛ cup garlic-flavored extra
  virgin olive oil

4 tablespoons ricotta cheese
8 teaspoons Parmesan cheese
4 tablespoons mozzarella
  cheese
1 cup marinara sauce

Sprinkle salt on each slice of eggplant. Place on plate and cover with another plate for 25 minutes. Squeeze and drain eggplant; pat dry. Dip slices in egg wash and bread crumbs. Sauté in oil. Set aside.

Dice remaining 2 slices eggplant and sauté in oil until well done, about 15 minutes. Set aside to cool. On each eggplant slice, place 1 tablespoon ricotta, diced eggplant, and 1 teaspoon Parmesan. Top with another slice of eggplant matched in size, and place in saucepan. Repeat process with remaining slices. Cover with marinara sauce, and to each portion add 1 teaspoon mozzarella and remainder of Parmesan cheese. Place in 350° oven until cheese melts and sauce starts to bubble.

Note: Salting and squeezing eggplant helps remove that slightly bitter taste. Always begin with this important step. Save the larger slices of eggplant for serving and the smaller end slices for the filling.

Cooking Italian in Hawaii

With 312 endangered plants and animals listed by the U.S. Fish and Wildlife Service, Hawai'i is home to the highest number of endangered species in the United States. California is second with 288.

Vegetarian Stir-Fry

1 bundle long rice
5 dried shiitake mushrooms
1 small head cauliflower,
  broken into florets
10–12 ounces tofu
3–4 tablespoons oil
1 stalk lemon grass, bulbous
  part only, minced
1 leek, white part only, sliced
1 carrot, thinly sliced

½ cup thinly sliced bamboo
  shoots
1 cup thinly sliced string beans
¼ cup water or vegetable
  broth
2 teaspoons sugar
3 tablespoons soy sauce
1 teaspoon nuoc mam (fish
  sauce)

Soak long rice in warm water for 30 minutes. Soak mushrooms in water. Blanch the cauliflower in boiling water; drain and set aside. Slice tofu into 4 pieces; heat some oil in a skillet and fry the tofu until brown. Drain on paper towels and when cool, slice into thin strips.

In the same skillet, heat some oil and stir-fry the lemon grass and leek for about 30 seconds. Add cauliflower and carrot; cook one minute. Add bamboo shoots and string beans, and stir-fry one minute. Drain long rice and cut into 3-inch lengths; drain mushrooms and slice thinly. Add the mushrooms, tofu, and long rice and stir in the water (or vegetable broth), sugar, soy sauce, and nuoc mam. Cook 1–2 minutes. Serves 4–6.

Ethnic Foods of Hawai'i

Vegetarian Loaf

1 cup finely chopped onion
1 cup finely chopped celery
1 cup finely chopped walnuts
1 cup shredded carrots
1 cup fine, dry, whole-wheat
  bread crumbs

½ teaspoon salt
½ teaspoon lemon pepper
¼ teaspoon celery seeds
2 eggs, slightly beaten
½ cup mayonnaise

Line a 8½x2½-inch loaf pan with foil; if using glass pan, grease pan instead of using foil. In a large bowl, stir together all ingredients except eggs and mayonnaise. In a small bowl, stir eggs and mayonnaise until well mixed, then fold into other ingredients. Pour into prepared pan. Bake at 350° for 50 minutes.

Note: Loaf will keep. Good to slice cold for sandwiches.

We, the Women of Hawaii Cookbook

Tofu Steak with Three Colored Bell Peppers

½ cup soy sauce
½ cup mirin
1 medium size onion, peeled
  and cut
½ ounce ginger, peeled and
  sliced
1 block firm tofu, sliced in
  thirds

Flour for dusting
Vegetable oil for frying
Unsalted butter for sautéing
1 pack enoki mushrooms,
  cleaned
1 each: red, yellow, and orange
  bell peppers, julienned
1 scallion, finely chopped

In an electric blender, combine soy sauce, mirin, onion, and ginger. Blend for 30 seconds until smooth, and set aside. Dust tofu with flour. In a large frying pan, heat vegetable oil and fry tofu until light brown on both sides. Remove from heat.

In frying pan, melt butter; add mushrooms and bell peppers and sauté until mushrooms wilt; set aside and keep warm. Place tofu slices on medium serving plate. Pour sauce over tofu and top with bell pepper mixture. Sprinkle with scallions. Serve immediately. Serves 2–4.

Kailua Cooks

Sukiyaki

6–8 shiitake mushrooms
(half-dollar size), slivered
2 cups water, divided
1 medium round onion or
green onions, slivered
1 teaspoon sesame oil
Pinch sea salt
¼ cup low-sodium soy sauce
2–4 tablespoons maple syrup
1½ cups bamboo shoots

1 (3-ounce) package cellophane
noodles, soaked in 2 cups
boiling water
2–3 carrots, sliced into
matchsticks
4 cups watercress
2–3 cups mung bean sprouts
4 cups won bok cabbage
½ block tofu (about 6 ounces)

Rinse the shiitake mushrooms and soak in 1 cup of water. Save the water for sukiyaki stock.

Sauté slivered onions and slivered mushrooms in remaining 1 cup water and sesame oil. Sprinkle some sea salt to prevent sticking. Add mushroom water and season to taste with low-sodium soy sauce and maple syrup. Add bamboo shoots to mixture, bring to a boil, and simmer at a low boil. Add soaked and drained cellophane noodles to mixture. Sprinkle julienned carrots. Layer watercress, bean sprouts, won bok, and tofu. Cover and allow layers of vegetables to be steamed. Makes 6–8 portions.

One portion: 173.2 calories; 3.1g fat; 15% fat; 18% protein; 67% carbohydrates

Eat More, Weigh Less Cookbook

Holiday Stuffed Butternut Squash

2 butternut squash
2 cups cooked brown rice
1 cup chopped onions
½ cup chopped celery
½ cup chopped bell pepper
½ teaspoon dried basil
1 teaspoon dried oregano
½ teaspoon herb seasoning
½ teaspoon cumin powder

2 tablespoons tamari or
  substitute
½ teaspoon garlic powder
½ teaspoon onion powder
1 cup chopped walnuts
½ cup chopped pecans
3 tablespoons tahini
3 slices toast

Slice butternuts in half and scoop out the seeds. Bake in a pre-heated oven at 350° for 20–30 minutes, until tender. Remove from oven and let cool. Carefully scoop out insides without breaking shells. Mix squash with rice. Save shells.

Sauté vegetables, then add them to squash-rice mixture. Add seasonings, nuts, and tahini. Slice the toast into small squares like croutons and add to mix. Stuff mixture into hollowed squash shells. Bake for another 20 minutes and serve with gravy. Serves 4.

Incredibly Delicious

Zucchini Lover's Casserole

6 medium zucchini, sliced
1 medium brown onion,
  chopped
3 medium carrots, grated
2 sticks butter (or less),
  divided

1 pint sour cream
2 (10¾-ounce) cans cream of
  mushroom soup, undiluted
8 ounces herbed croutons,
  crumbled, divided

Preheat oven to 375°. Steam zucchini until tender and drain. Sauté onion and carrots in one stick of butter until soft. Mix sour cream with undiluted soup, and add zucchini, carrots, and onions. Stir in ½ of the croutons. Put into a buttered 9x13-inch baking dish. Cover with remaining croutons and dot with butter. Bake 45 minutes or until golden on top.

Shaloha Cookbook

Baked Broccoli

1–2 pounds broccoli
2 (10¾-ounce) cans cream of
    mushroom soup, divided
1 package imitation crabmeat

½ cup grated Cheddar cheese
½ cup grated Monterey Jack
    cheese
½ cup mozzarella cheese

Cut broccoli into bite-size pieces. Parboil slightly until crunchy. Layer into 9x13-inch pan the broccoli, 1 can soup, crabmeat, other can soup, then top with mixed cheeses. Bake in 325° oven until cheese melts.

Favorite Island Cookery Book IV

Gingered Carrots

2 pounds carrots
¾ stick butter
2 tablespoons finely grated,
    fresh ginger

2 tablespoons honey
Salt and pepper to taste

Peel carrots, cut in thin slices, and steam till tender. In large frying pan, melt butter, add grated ginger, and fry briefly. Stir in honey, salt and pepper to taste, then toss in the carrots just to glaze them—about 2 minutes. Serve hot. Serves 8.

Hawaii Cooks Throughout the Year

Having produced a lava flow since January 1983, Kilauea, on the island of Hawai'i, is the longest continuously erupting volcano in recorded history. The Hawaiian name "Kilauea" means "spewing" or "much spreading."

Snow Peas Kahala Style

12–14 water chestnuts, sliced
 ¼-inch thick
1 cup thinly sliced, fresh
 mushrooms
1 cup diced onion
2 tablespoons peanut oil
¾ pound fresh snow peas, or
 3 (6-ounce) packages frozen
 Chinese snow peas

1 teaspoon salt
1 tablespoon soy sauce
1 tablespoon water
½ teaspoon garlic salt

In a wok or large skillet with a tight fitting cover, sauté water chestnuts, mushrooms, and onion in peanut oil for 5 minutes or until onion is tender. Add snow peas, salt, soy sauce, and water. Mix well. Sprinkle with garlic salt. Cover tightly and simmer 5 minutes or until snow peas are tender but still crisp. Serves 4–6.

A Taste of Aloha

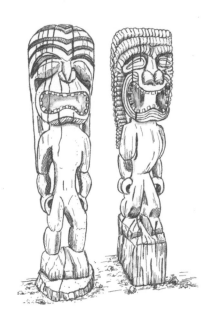

Rice, Pasta, Etc.

Years of the sea eroding away at lava rock created the unique Holei Sea Arch in Volcanoes National Park on the big island of Hawai'i.

Vietnamese-Style Fried Rice

1 large egg plus 1 large
egg white, beaten
1 tablespoon vegetable oil,
divided
3 cloves garlic, chopped
½ cup chopped green
onions, white parts only
1 medium onion, chopped
½ large, red bell pepper,
seeded, finely chopped
1 large carrot, peeled, grated
1 Thai bird chile pepper,
sliced

Pinch red pepper flakes
2 tablespoons soy sauce
1 tablespoon patis (fish sauce)
1 tablespoon rice wine vinegar
1 tablespoon Thai chili garlic
paste
4 cups cooked jasmine rice (air
dried or refrigerated)
1½ cups bean sprouts
¼ cup chopped green onions,
green parts only
¼ cup chopped cilantro
¼ cup chopped peanuts

In a wok over medium heat, scramble eggs in a teaspoon of oil.
Remove from wok; reserve. Into wok, stir-fry garlic, onions, bell
pepper, carrot, and chile pepper in remaining oil. Add pepper
flakes, soy sauce, patis, vinegar, and chili garlic paste. Add rice
and eggs; heat through. Remove from heat. Stir in bean
sprouts, green onions, cilantro, and peanuts. Serves 3.

Variation: Add ground pork or fishcake (used as substitute for crab,
scallops, etc.). Substitute scrambled soft tofu for eggs.

Dd's Table Talk II

Rice Ramen Curry

1 pot cooked brown rice
1 package low-fat ramen
  noodles
1 tablespoon curry powder

1 cup chopped Chinese
  parsley
½ cup raisins

While rice is cooking, break up the ramen noodles while still in package with the heel of the hand until there are no large chunks. Open package, remove spice package, and mix crushed noodles with the cooked brown rice. (The heat of the rice cooks the noodles.) Add the spice packet, curry powder, parsley, and raisins. Ready to serve hot or cold.

A Race for Life

Spicy Fried Rice

This is not a recipe to be forgotten; taste it once and you'll make it again and again. Cook the rice for this dish in advance; it fries best when it's had a chance to cool.

3 tablespoons mild oil, such
  as canola
2 cups finely chopped onions
¾ teaspoon salt
1 tablespoon ume plum
  vinegar
1 tablespoon soy sauce
1–2 teaspoons Tabasco sauce

6 tablespoons tomato paste
Scant ½ cup chopped scallions
¾ cup finely chopped Chinese
  parsley, divided
4 cups cooked rice
1 ripe tomato, cut in wedges,
  for garnish

Heat oil in a wok or large frying pan. When it's hot, add onions and cook until transparent. Combine salt, vinegar, soy sauce, Tabasco, tomato paste, scallions, and ½ cup of the Chinese parsley; set aside.

Add rice to wok; stir-fry 3 minutes. Add tomato paste mixture and stir-fry 5 minutes on high heat. Turn the rice onto a serving platter. Garnish with the remaining Chinese parsley and tomato wedges. Serve immediately. Yields 4–5 servings.

Vegetarian Nights

Fried Rice

3 strips bacon, chopped
1½ cups diced ham, leftover
  beef, hot dogs or other meat
3 cups cooked rice (leftover
  cold rice is fine)

1 egg
1 tablespoon shoyu
3 stalks green onions, minced

Cook bacon in skillet until it is crisp. Drain most of the fat. Add diced meat of your choice to the pan and cook for 2 minutes. Turn heat to low and add rice. Place egg and shoyu in a small bowl or cup and mix with a fork. Add it to the meat and rice. Add minced onions last. Continue to cook for 2–3 minutes or until slightly set. Serves 4.

Aunty Pua's Keiki Cookbook

Spam Fried Rice

Good with fried eggs.

1½ cups diced Spam
Leftover rice, about 4 cups
  (cooked)

1 egg
1 tablespoon shoyu
3 stalks green onions, chopped

Fry Spam in a bit of oil in a skillet. Turn heat to low and add rice. Mix egg with shoyu and add to the rice and Spam. Add chopped green onions just before serving.

Hawai'i's Spam Cookbook

 Hawaiians consume some 4.3 million cans of Spam a year. Spam was introduced to the islands during World War II when military personnel brought it with them from the mainland.

Cheese and Rice Soufflé

1½ cups white sauce
Salt and paprika to taste
1¼ cups grated Cheddar
  cheese

1½ cups cooked rice
2 eggs, separated
⅛ teaspoon baking powder

Season white sauce highly with salt and paprika. Add cheese and heat slowly until cheese is melted. Add rice and beaten egg yolks. Cool slightly. Fold in stiffly beaten egg whites. Add baking powder. Pour into well-buttered soufflé pan set in pan of hot water. Bake in preheated 350° oven for 30 minutes.

We, the Women of Hawaii Cookbook

Green Rice

1 cup cooked rice
1½ cups grated sharp cheese
1 cup milk
1 egg, slightly beaten
½ medium onion, chopped

½ teaspoon salt
1 (10-ounce) box frozen
  spinach, thawed and
  well drained
¼ cup butter, melted

Preheat oven to 350°. Combine ingredients and pour into greased 1½-quart casserole dish. Cover. Bake 40 minutes. Serves 4.

Kailua Cooks

Macadamia-Pineapple Rice Pilaf

1 tablespoon unsalted butter
1 ½ cups long-grain white rice
2 teaspoons minced garlic
1 medium white onion, diced
¼ red bell pepper, seeded
  and diced
¼ yellow bell pepper, seeded
  and diced
3 cups strong chicken stock

½ cup golden raisins
½ cup chopped macadamia
  nuts
1 fresh sage leaf
Salt to taste
⅓ cup chopped fresh cilantro
1 cup diced pineapple, reserve
  juice

Preheat oven to 375°. In a flame-proof casserole, melt butter on medium-high heat and add rice. Stir for a few seconds until rice is coated, but not long enough to let rice change color. Add garlic, onion, and red and yellow bell peppers, and cook for a few more seconds. Add chicken stock and bring mixture to a gentle boil. Add raisins, nuts, sage, and salt. Cover and place in oven and bake for 30 minutes. Remove dish from oven and let it rest (without uncovering) for another 10 minutes. Add the cilantro and pineapple bits. Season if necessary and serve at once.

Note: May mix chicken stock and syrup from pineapple to make up the 3 cups of liquid needed. If using salted macadamia nuts, remember to adjust seasonings.

Tropical Taste

Peking Pasta

1 onion, chopped
4 cloves garlic, chopped
1 tablespoon butter
3 tablespoons peanut oil
¾ pound ground pork
1 teaspoon sugar
1½ tablespoons soy sauce
1 tablespoon hoisin sauce
1 tablespoon red miso paste

2 tablespoons dry sherry
2 tablespoons water
1 pound spaghetti, cooked
    according to package
    directions
Julienne cucumbers, green
    onions, and bean sprouts for
    garnish

In a large skillet over medium-high heat, sauté onion and garlic in butter and oil. Add pork and stir-fry for 3 minutes. Add remaining ingredients except spaghetti; simmer for 5 minutes. Serve over spaghetti with garnishes. Serves 6–8.

Dd's Table Talk

Quick and Simple Spaghetti with Clam Sauce

1 clove garlic, minced
1 medium onion, chopped
Olive oil
2 (8-ounce) cans diced
    tomatoes
2 small cans chopped clams
    (reserve juice of one can)
1 (8-ounce) can tomato sauce

1 (6-ounce) can tomato paste
1 level teaspoon parsley flakes
⅛ teaspoon oregano
1 teaspoon basil
1 teaspoon sugar
Salt and pepper to taste
1 cup red wine
Pasta of your choice, cooked

Sauté garlic and onion in olive oil. Add diced tomatoes and bring to a boil. Add clams with liquid from one can only. Add tomato sauce and stir in tomato paste to thicken. Add seasonings and wine; bring to a boil and simmer for 20 minutes. Pour over pasta and serve with French bread and wine.

Recipe by HFD Chief Attilio K. Leonardi
Hawai'i's Favorite Firehouse Recipes

Thai Chicken Angel Hair

2 boneless, skinless chicken
   breasts, cut in strips
Salt and freshly ground
   black pepper
Flour for dredging
1 tablespoon plus ¼ cup
   peanut oil, divided
¼ cup sesame seed oil
3 tablespoons Thai fried garlic,
   or 3 cloves garlic, chopped
1 small Hawaiian chili pepper,
   seeded and chopped

2 tablespoons mirin sake
8 ounces angel hair pasta,
   cooked according to package
   directions
1 tablespoon fish sauce
1 tablespoon pickled ginger
3 tablespoons each: chopped
   fresh basil, mint leaves, and
   cilantro
3 tablespoons chopped, toasted
   peanuts
Juice and zest of 1 grated lime

Lightly season chicken with salt and pepper; dredge in flour. In a small skillet over medium-high heat, brown chicken in one tablespoon of peanut oil. Drain on paper towels and set aside.

In a small saucepan, heat remaining oils, garlic, chili pepper, and mirin sake. Combine cooked pasta, chicken, oil mixture, and remaining ingredients. Season to taste. Serves 4.

Dd's Table Talk

Chicken Linguine

1 pound fresh chicken,
   julienned
4 tablespoons garlic-flavored,
   extra virgin olive oil
1 carrot, peeled and julienned
1 each: red and green bell
   pepper, seeded and julienned

½ pound sliced mushrooms
½ zucchini, julienned (skin on)
Kosher salt
Freshly ground black pepper
1 tablespoon dried basil
1 pound linguine
2 teaspoons Romano cheese

Sauté chicken 5–10 minutes in olive oil. Add carrot and sauté 4–5 minutes. Add bell peppers, mushrooms, and zucchini. Sprinkle with salt, pepper, and basil. Cook linguine in 2 quarts boiling water. Toss cooked linguine in pan with chicken and vegetables. Sprinkle with Romano cheese and serve immediately.

Cooking Italian in Hawaii

Green Chile Pesto

I first tasted Green Chile Pesto on a fabulous veggie burger at Maui Coffee Roasters in Kahului. Owner Nick Matichyn uses macadamia nuts in his pesto; I've substituted pine nuts because they're more widely available. The concept of chiles in pesto was totally foreign to me until the moment it kissed my lips. What a taste!

7 ounces (about 1 cup) canned
  green chiles, chopped
2 cloves garlic
½ cup pine nuts (or chopped
  macadamia nuts)

1 cup Chinese parsley or
  basil leaves, packed into
  measuring cup
¼ cup extra virgin olive oil
1 teaspoon salt

Blenderize everything using the pulse feature on the blender. Don't aim for a totally smooth paste; it's good to retain some of the texture of the nuts.

This pesto is great on sandwiches and as a topping for pasta, steamed vegetables, grains, and baked potatoes. Yields 3–4 servings (more than 1½ cups, or enough to top 8 ounces of pasta).

Vegetarian Nights

Broccoli Pesto

We use this as a dressing for pasta salad; it is also great tossed with hot pasta!

4 cups broccoli
1 cup chicken stock, divided
4 cloves garlic
1 cup tightly packed basil

¼ cup almonds
¼ cup Parmesan cheese
⅛ teaspoon salt

Steam broccoli. Add 6 tablespoons stock to broccoli. In food processor, add garlic, basil, and almonds, and process until finely chopped. Add 2 tablespoons stock, then add broccoli, Parmesan, salt, and remaining liquid. Process until very smooth, scraping the sides frequently. Makes 2½ cups.

Friends and Celebrities Cookbook II

Super Macaroni and Cheese

Little kids love this dish.

1 (7-ounce) box macaroni and
  cheese dinner
3 tablespoons butter
2 cloves garlic, minced
1 cup sliced mushrooms

½ can Spam luncheon meat,
  cubed
Grated Cheddar cheese
  (optional)

Prepare macaroni and cheese according to directions on box. Melt butter in skillet. Add garlic, mushrooms, and cubed Spam, and cook until mushrooms are soft (if using fresh ones). Add mushrooms and Spam to prepared macaroni and cheese. Place in casserole dish and sprinkle top with additional grated cheese, if desired. Bake for 25–30 minutes in 350° oven. Serves 3–4.

Hawai'i's 2nd Spam Cookbook

A tsunami is a series of waves traveling across the ocean with extremely long wavelengths of up to hundreds of miles between wave crests. Often a tsunami is incorrectly referred to as a tidal wave. Tidal waves are associated with the rise and fall of the tides produced by the gravitational attraction of the sun and moon. Tsunamis are usually the result of a sudden rise or fall of a section of the earth's crust under or near the ocean.

This century, thirteen significant tsunamis have impacted Hawai'i. The most destructive took place on April 1, 1946, resulting in 159 deaths. That morning an earthquake with a reported magnitude of 7.1 occurred in the Aleutian Islands off of Alaska. Almost five hours later, the largest and most destructive tsunami waves in reported history struck the Hawaiian Islands. Maximum runups were reported to be 54 feet in Moloka'i, and 55 feet in Pololu Valley on the Big Island. Waves in some areas penetrated more than half a mile inland. Between wave crests, the drawdown is reported to have exposed some areas of the seafloor 500 feet in the seaward direction.

Meats

Within hours during the attack on Pearl Harbor, 2,390 service men and women lost their lives; 1,177 of these casualties were from the battleship U.S.S. Arizona. Completed in 1961, the 184-foot-long U.S.S. Arizona Memorial was built over the remains of the sunken battleship.

Okinawan Pot Roast Pork

1 (4- to 5-pound) lean pork butt

SAUCE:

2 cups soy sauce	½ cup mirin
½ cup water	1 (1-inch) piece ginger, crushed
2½ cups sugar	1–2 cloves garlic, crushed

Combine Sauce ingredients in a large saucepan; mix well and marinate pork overnight in the refrigerator.

Cover and cook over high heat until Sauce comes to a boil. Lower heat and continue cooking, turning meat over occasionally for 3–4 hours, or until meat is tender. Make and add more Sauce, if necessary. Serves 6–8.

West Kauai's Plantation Heritage

Oven Kalua Pig

2 tablespoons Hawaiian salt	1 (½-inch) slice ginger,
¼ cup soy sauce	crushed
1 teaspoon Worcestershire	1 tablespoon liquid smoke
sauce	1 (4- to 5-pound) pork butt
2 cloves garlic, crushed	Ti or banana leaves

Mix together salt, soy sauce, Worcestershire sauce, garlic, ginger, and liquid smoke. Place pork on several ti or banana leaves. Rub with seasonings and let stand one hour. Fold leaves over to wrap the pork. Wrap the leaf-enclosed pork in foil. Place in a baking pan and bake in a 325° oven for 4–5 hours. Unwrap pork, cool, and shred meat. Serves 8–10.

Ethnic Foods of Hawai'i

Kalua pig is a popular dish in Hawai'i, often served at lū'aus. "Kalua" means "the pit" in Hawaiian and refers to the method the pig is cooked— in an underground earthen oven called an imu.

Four Peppercorn Pork Roast

1 (4½-pound) boneless pork
loin, tied
Salt to taste
3 tablespoons unsalted butter,
softened
¼ cup plus 2 tablespoons
flour, divided

¼ cup mixed peppercorns,
very coarsely crushed
1¾ cups chicken broth
1 cup water
2 tablespoons red wine vinegar
Fresh rosemary for garnish

Preheat oven to 475°. Season roast with salt. Combine butter
and 2 tablespoons of flour to make a paste. Spread the top of
the roast with the paste. Lightly press peppercorns into butter
paste. Place pork on a rack in a roasting pan. Roast at 475° for
30 minutes. Reduce heat to 325° and continue roasting for
1½–1⅔ hours, or until meat thermometer registers 155°.

Transfer roast to cutting board and let stand for 10 minutes.
Prepare sauce while roast is standing. Pour all but ¼ cup of fat
from roasting pan. Whisk in ¼ cup flour and cook over mod-
erate heat for 3 minutes, stirring constantly. Slowly stir in the
chicken broth and water. Bring to a boil. Stir in red wine vinegar and salt to taste. Simmer sauce until thickened to desired
consistency. Remove string from the roast and cut into ½-inch
slices. Arrange on platter with sauce and garnish with fresh
rosemary. Serves 8–10.

Another Taste of Aloha

Easy Beef Stroganoff

1½ pounds top sirloin, cubed
½–1 pound mushrooms,
 sliced
1 large onion, diced
2 tablespoons oil
1 (10½-ounce) can beef
 consommé

2 tablespoons flour
1 cup sour cream
Salt and pepper to taste
1 (8-ounce) package egg
 noodles, cooked

Sauté cubed beef, mushrooms, and onion in oil until soft and the meat is browned. Add consommé and simmer for 20 minutes. Mix flour with sour cream. Add to beef mixture. Heat, but do not boil, until thickened. Add salt and pepper to taste. Serve over egg noodles. Yields 4 servings.

Seasoned with Aloha Vol. 2

Easy Local Ribs

Oven braise is a local favorite—sweet and sour spareribs packed with pineapple.

3 pounds meaty, country-style,
 pork spareribs, cut in pieces
3 tablespoons soy sauce
1 teaspoon salt

Dash pepper
Pineapple chunks
Green onions, chopped

Rub spareribs all over with soy sauce, salt, and pepper. Place ribs, meat-side-up in a foil-lined shallow baking or roasting pan, and cover with foil or baking-pan lid. Bake 20–25 minutes at 450°. Drain off fat. Makes 4 servings.

SAUCE:
1 cup syrup-packed pineapple
 chunks, drained
½ cup packed brown sugar
⅓ cup ketchup

⅓ cup vinegar
2 tablespoons soy sauce
2 teaspoons grated fresh ginger
2 cloves garlic, minced

Combine Sauce ingredients; pour over ribs. Bake at 350° for 1 hour or until tender, basting occasionally. Garnish with pineapple chunks and green onions.

Sam Choy's Sampler

Barbecued Shortribs

5 pounds meaty shortribs,
  cut in 2-inch pieces
Salt and pepper to taste
Flour
2 medium onions, sliced
2 teaspoons vinegar
2 tablespoons Worcestershire
  sauce

1 tablespoon salt
1 teaspoon paprika
1 teaspoon chili powder
¾ cup tomato catsup
½ teaspoon cayenne pepper
½ teaspoon black pepper
  (optional)
¾ cup water

Sprinkle shortribs with salt and pepper to taste; dredge in flour. Place in a roaster and cover with onions. Combine remaining ingredients; mix well and pour over shortribs. Cover and bake at 350° for 3 hours, basting occasionally, and turning meat over once or twice during baking. Remove cover during last 15 minutes of baking. Serves 6–8.

Note: This can be cooked a day or two ahead and refrigerated. Remove and discard solidified grease before reheating to serve.

The Tastes and Tales of Moiliili

Unlike the volcanic craters on the Big Island, Haleakala Crater is an erosion crater. Its last eruption in 1790 filled enormous canyons and raised the summit floor. An awesome playground for the adventurous, Haleakala Crater is vast and desolate . . . and awesomely beautiful.

Laulau

2 pounds stew meat (pork,
  beef, chicken, or
  combination)
2 pounds pork belly
½ cup Hawaiian salt (or
  rock salt)

Several large ti leaves
1 bunch taro leaves, or fresh
  leaf spinach
String for tying bundles

Cut meat and pork belly into chunks, then mix in salt. Clean ti leaves and trim off back ribs so they'll be flexible. Wrap a piece of pork belly and a piece of meat (or chicken) in 3 or 4 taro or spinach leaves. Cross 2 ti leaves at right angles. Roll up meat and taro leaves one way in first ti leaf, then crossways with the other, and tie bundle tightly. Put in steamer and steam 4–5 hours.

Note: Heavy aluminum foil may be substituted for ti leaves, but the flavor won't be quite the same.

West Kauai's Plantation Heritage

In Volcanoes National Park on the Big Island, hiking trails take you where molten lava has destroyed most everything in its path. In time, little specks of green began to spring forth, beginning life's cycle once again. Though walking through this barren area is desolate and a little eerie, it has a special beauty all its own.

Polynesian Style Brisket

Polynesian flavors seem to blend perfectly in this brisket recipe. This is a wonderful dinner for company, as it cooks without any fuss in the oven. It may even be made a day ahead. This method of cooking with a foil cover keeps all the flavorful juices captured inside the pan. Just be sure to carefully tuck the foil around the pan so you retain a sealed cover without any breaks. You might want to double the recipe and have an extra brisket for a picnic. It is also marvelous cold.

1 (4- to 5-pound) beef brisket
1 cup soy sauce
½ cup dry sherry
½ cup brown sugar
1 cup orange, lemon, or
   pineapple juice
2 cloves garlic, peeled and
   minced

Salt and pepper to taste
2 tablespoons freshly grated
   ginger (or 1 tablespoon
   dried)
1 cup fresh or canned
   pineapple, diced (for garnish)

Place brisket in a bowl or shallow pan. Mix together remaining ingredients, except garnish, and pour over the brisket. Make sure all parts of the meat are covered. Refrigerate at least 4 hours, or preferably overnight.

Place brisket in a baking pan with marinade. Cover tightly with a double layer of foil. Bake at 325° for 3½ hours. Check during baking to make sure there is enough liquid; if not, add extra soy sauce or fruit juice, being sure to replace the foil tightly.

To serve, remove meat from juices. Slice and serve with warmed pan juices and pineapple on top. This will serve 4–5. In Honolulu, rice is usually served with the brisket.

Honolulu Hawaii Cooking

Covering half the Big Island of Hawai'i, Mauna Loa is the largest active volcano on the earth, with an elevation of 13,680 feet above sea level and a summit about 56,000 feet above its ocean floor base. With its most recent eruption in 1984, Mauna Loa is also among the earth's most active volcanoes, having erupted 33 times since its first well-documented eruption in 1843. The Hawaiian name "Mauna Loa" means "long mountain."

Marinated Beef for 10 or More

A party pleaser.

1 (5-pound) rump roast (long cut,
   not triangle cut)

Start recipe 24 hours before serving. Cook rump roast at 325° for
4 hours for medium well, less for rare. Cool and slice thinly.

SAUCE:

¼ cup vinegar
1½ cups water
½ cup sugar
4 teaspoons prepared mustard
½ cup catsup
¼ teaspoon cayenne pepper
¼ teaspoon black pepper

1 teaspoon salt
3 teaspoons Worcestershire
   sauce
¼ cup red wine (optional)
¼ cup light soy sauce
2 medium Maui onions, sliced
2 slices lemon (very important)

Mix all Sauce ingredients. Place meat slices in a large pan, over-
lapping diagonally. Pour marinade over meat, making sure
Sauce gets between slices. Cover and refrigerate for 24 hours.
Bake at 325° for 1 hour under aluminum tent.

Cook 'em Up Kaua'i

Hawaiian Teriyaki Burger

This is definitely a local favorite.

1½ pounds ground beef
1 small onion, chopped
1 egg
¼ cup shoyu
¼ cup sugar

2 cloves garlic, minced
½ teaspoon minced fresh
   ginger
2 stalks green onions, chopped
1 tablespoon sesame oil

Combine all ingredients; mix well. Form into patties. Fry, grill,
or broil.

Hawai'i's Best Local Dishes

Lazy Loco Moco

1 tablespoon oil	1 cup hot water
1 pound ground beef	2 tablespoons cornstarch
1 clove garlic, minced	2 tablespoons cold water
3 tablespoons shoyu	4 eggs
2 stalks green onions, chopped	3 cups hot cooked rice

In a large skillet, heat oil and brown beef with the garlic. Add shoyu, green onions, and hot water. Let mixture come to a boil and cook 2–3 minutes. Mix cornstarch with cold water and add to the beef mixture. Cook until sauce thickens. Reduce heat to simmer.

Using a large spoon, make 4 holes in the beef mixture and break an egg into each hole. Cover and cook until eggs are cooked the way you like them. Serve the beef-egg mixture over hot rice. Serves 4.

Aunty Pua's Keiki Cookbook

Loco moco is Hawai'i's original homemade fast food and can be found at just about any fast food restaurant, roadside diner, or lunch wagon. Legend has it the dish was created in Hilo on the island of Hawai'i in 1949 by the owners of the Lincoln Grill, Mr. and Mrs. Inouye. Their goal was to create a fast, easy dish for hungry teenaged customers. So they took a bowl, spooned in two scoops of rice, a hamburger, and a fried egg, and then topped it with brown gravy. Today, the loco moco basics are two scoops of rice, a big burger or two regulars, an over-easy egg, and brown beef gravy. Usually it is accompanied by a scoop of macaroni salad on the side.

Arabian Night's Delite

1 pound ground beef
1 tablespoon butter or margarine
1 small round onion, chopped
4 full sprigs parsley, chopped fine
1 teaspoon salt
½ teaspoon pepper
1 teaspoon cinnamon
5 eggs
1 (10-ounce) box frozen, chopped spinach, thawed, and drained
1 box filo leaves (approximately 12 leaves in a box)

Fry ground beef in butter. Add onion, parsley, salt, pepper, and cinnamon. Drain and set mixture aside in a bowl. Beat eggs in a bowl and add spinach, stirring lightly. Fry eggs-spinach mixture in a large frying pan, turning over carefully so that the omelet is flat. Slide it out from the pan onto a large platter; slice into rectangles about 1½ x ¾ inches in size, and set aside.

Assemble the following items in a cool part of the kitchen or dining room (so that the filo leaves won't dry out so quickly): beef and egg mixtures, large tray on which to put the rolled Delites, a large pastry board on which to roll the pastry, a small sharp knife, a tablespoon, and the filo leaves. Then, carefully unpack the leaves (detailed instructions are on the box) and lightly cover them with a slightly damp towel to prevent them from drying out and becoming too brittle to roll nicely.

Carefully take a filo leaf and cut it in half. For each Delite, use a half sheet and place about 2 tablespoons ground beef at the bottom of the strip, and put an egg rectangle on top. Fold the bottom of the filo over the filling, rolling twice, then fold the left and right edges of the filo over about ½ inch. Roll up the filo leaf to the end. Place roll seam-side-down on the large tray. Continue making rolls until all the filling is used. Deep-fry each roll until golden brown. Drain on paper towels. Serve. Serves 6–8 people.

Note: To prevent seam from separating when frying, seal the roll with a dab or two of water.

Friends and Celebrities Cookbook II

Veal Anna O'Neal

4 slices peeled eggplant, cut
  lengthwise, salted, rinsed
Flavored bread crumbs
Egg wash (one beaten egg)
¼ cup garlic-flavored extra
  virgin olive oil
1 pound mushrooms, sliced

4 (6-ounce) scallopine of veal
½ cup mozzarella cheese
4 teaspoons Parmesan cheese,
  divided
20 ounces marinara sauce if
  served without pasta (1 quart
  with pasta)

Preheat oven to 400°. Dredge eggplant in egg wash and bread crumbs. In a cast-iron skillet, sauté in oil. Set aside.

Sauté mushrooms over low heat; set aside. Dredge veal scallopine in egg wash and bread crumbs. Sauté and set aside.

In a baking dish brushed with olive oil, layer veal, eggplant, marinara sauce, and 1 teaspoon Parmesan per serving. (Just use skillet as baking pan if preparing for fewer than 4 people.) Bake until cheese melts over top and sauce bubbles. Serve with pasta.

Cooking Italian in Hawaii

Lamb Shanks Roasted in Red Wine

¼ cup oil
2 onions, sliced thin
3 cloves garlic, minced
4 carrots, sliced thin
2 celery stalks, sliced thin
1 bay leaf, crushed
3 sprigs fresh oregano or 1
   teaspoon dried

3 sprigs fresh rosemary
½ cup chopped parsley
1½ cups dry red wine
1 (10½-ounce) can tomato
   sauce
Salt and freshly ground pepper
6 lamb shanks, trimmed of fat
8 mushrooms, sliced thinly

Heat oil in large roasting pan and sauté onions and garlic until tender. Add carrots, celery, bay leaf, oregano, rosemary, parsley, wine, and tomato sauce. Simmer. Season to taste with salt and pepper. Add lamb shanks and baste with sauce.

Cover and cook in a 375° oven 1½–2 hours, basting every 20 minutes. Uncover, add mushrooms, and cook additional 30 minutes or until shanks are tender, turning shanks to keep moist. Arrange lamb shanks on a large platter with vegetables and sauce. Serves 6.

Shaloha Cookbook

Poultry

'Iolani Palace is the only royal palace on American soil. King David Kalākaua built the Palace in 1882. After the Hawaiian government was overthrown, it became the capitol building and now serves as a museum.

Baked Guava Chicken

12 small chicken breasts, or
  5 pounds chicken parts
1 (10-ounce) jar guava jelly
1 tablespoon cornstarch
1 cup water
½ cup lemon juice

1½ teaspoons Worcestershire
  sauce
¼ cup shoyu
1 teaspoon allspice
½ teaspoon Hawaiian salt
½ teaspoon white pepper

Place chicken in baking pan. Mix all other ingredients in a saucepan and simmer for 5 minutes. Pour over chicken. Bake in preheated 350° oven for 40 minutes to 1 hour. Baste frequently. Add water if necessary.

We, the Women of Hawaii Cookbook

Five Spices Shoyu Chicken

½ cup shoyu
½ cup water
2 teaspoons sugar
1 teaspoon oyster sauce
1 clove garlic, crushed

1 (1-inch) piece fresh ginger,
  grated
Dash of Chinese five-spice
  powder
3–4 pounds chicken

Bring to a boil all ingredients, except chicken. Add chicken to mixture and bring to a boil again. Lower heat and simmer 40–45 minutes, or until chicken is tender. Yields 6 servings.

Serving suggestion: Parboil 3 cups of Chinese cabbage cut into 1½-inch lengths. Drain and place on a serving platter. Place cooked chicken on Chinese cabbage. Add 3 tablespoons cornstarch mixed with 3 tablespoons water to sauce to thicken. Pour over chicken and garnish with Chinese parsley.

Hawai'i's Best Local Dishes

Sesame Chicken

6 chicken thighs, boned and
  cut into 1- to 1½-inch cubes
Cornstarch

Peanut oil
Chopped green onions for
  garnish

Coat chicken thoroughly with cornstarch and refrigerate for at least one hour. Coat again lightly just before frying. Deep-fry the chicken pieces in peanut oil at 350° for 3 minutes or until light golden brown. Drain and dip in Sauce. Serve over rice. Spoon on any unused Sauce and garnish with green onions. Serves 6.

SAUCE:

¼ cup soy sauce
¼ cup sugar
1 tablespoon sesame seeds,
  toasted

1 (1-inch) piece fresh ginger,
  finely grated
2 green onions, finely sliced
½–1 teaspoon sesame oil

In a saucepan, mix soy sauce, sugar, sesame seeds, and ginger. Cook over low heat until sugar is dissolved. Stir in green onions and sesame oil.

Another Taste of Aloha

Not your ordinary newspaperman, this one is a mime on the busy streets of Waikiki who beckons you to sit beside him and hold his hand. The dog, however, is not real.

Chicken Lū'au

2 cups coconut milk
2 pounds chicken
2 tablespoons oil
2 cloves garlic, crushed

1½ teaspoons salt, divided
2½ cups water, divided
2 pounds taro leaves (lū'au)

Prepare fresh coconut milk or use canned coconut milk. Cut chicken into bite-sized pieces. In saucepan, heat oil; add crushed garlic. Add chicken and brown. Sprinkle with 1 teaspoon salt and add 1 cup water. Cover and simmer until chicken is tender.

Wash taro leaves; remove tough stems. Place leaves in a pan with 1½ cups water and ½ teaspoon salt. Simmer, partially covered, for one hour. Drain and squeeze water out. Drain chicken; combine with lū'au leaves. Add coconut milk and bring to a boil. Serve immediately. Serves 4–6.

Note: Fresh spinach may be substituted if lū'au is not available.

Ethnic Foods of Hawai'i

Quick Chicken Lū'au

1 (10-ounce) package frozen
  leaf spinach
1 (10¾-ounce) can cream of
  chicken soup

8 chicken thighs (or breasts)
1 (12-ounce) can coconut milk

Thaw spinach by leaving it at room temperature for several hours, or defrost in the microwave (3–4 minutes). Squeeze water out of it, using your hands. Spread spinach out in a greased, 9x13-inch baking pan. Spread soup over it. Place chicken over the soup. Pour coconut milk over chicken. Bake in a 350° oven for one hour. Serves 4.

Note: Traditional chicken lū'au is made out of taro tops called lū'au leaves. Spinach is a quick substitute.

Aunty Pua's Keiki Cookbook

Pete's Roasted Teriyaki Chicken

Teriyaki is a classic island sauce used on everything from beef and chicken to fish.

1 cup shoyu	4 cloves garlic, peeled and
1 cup sugar	crushed
1 (3-inch) piece ginger, peeled	2 tablespoons bourbon
and sliced	1 (3½-pound) chicken

Cook the shoyu and sugar in a small saucepan over medium-low heat until sugar dissolves, about 2 minutes. Stir in ginger, garlic, and bourbon, and cook 30 minutes. Remove ginger and garlic. Pour ¼ cup of the sauce into a small mixing bowl and store the additional for later use. It will keep in the refrigerator for up to one week. Makes 2 cups sauce.

Preheat oven to 375°. Rinse chicken and pat dry. Tie the legs together with kitchen string. Using a brush, coat the chicken with sauce inside the cavity and out. Place chicken in a baking pan and roast for one hour, basting every 15 minutes. If you want a darker bird, baste more often. The chicken is done when you pierce the leg with a knife and the juice runs clear. Take the chicken out and allow it to rest for 15 minutes before carving. Serves 4.

Hawaiian Country Tables

The longest and deepest explored lava tube is Kazumura Cave, on the island of Hawai'i. It is 25 miles long and descends 3,600 feet down the eastern side of Kilauea volcano. Lava tubes are natural channels that lava travels through beneath the surface of a lava flow. Tubes form by the crusting over of lava flows.

Teri Chicken

½ cup sugar
⅔ cup shoyu
2 tablespoons water
3 cloves garlic, minced

1 thin slice fresh ginger, crushed
3 stalks green onions, chopped
4–5 pounds chicken pieces

In a mixing bowl, stir together all ingredients except chicken. Place chicken in baking pan and pour sauce over it. Place pan in the refrigerator and soak chicken for several hours or overnight.

When you are ready to cook, turn chicken over and place pan in a 325° oven for 1 hour and 15 minutes. During this time, turn chicken once, using tongs. If you prefer, chicken may be cooked outside on a charcoal grill. Serves 6–8.

Aunty Pua's Keiki Cookbook

Yaki Tori

¼ cup sugar
5 tablespoons shoyu
½ teaspoon salt
1 clove garlic, crushed

1 tablespoon sherry or sake
1 teaspoon sesame oil
2 pounds chicken thighs, deboned

Blend sugar, shoyu, salt, garlic, sherry, and sesame oil together. Soak chicken in sauce overnight.

Cook on charcoal grill, or skewer, if desired, with onion and green pepper, and broil or pan fry. Delicious either way. Double sauce if using more chicken.

Favorite Recipes for Islanders

Sweet Ginger Chicken

2 tablespoons honey
1½ cups orange juice
½ teaspoon grated orange
  peel
1 teaspoon minced garlic
⅛ teaspoon white pepper

1 tablespoon grated fresh
  ginger
4 whole skinless chicken
  breasts, cut in half
1 teaspoon cornstarch or flour

Mix honey into orange juice until well dissolved. Add all other ingredients except chicken and cornstarch, and mix well. Put marinade into a double plastic ZipLoc bag, add chicken, and place in bowl in refrigerator. Turn bag to coat chicken a few times while marinating.

Take chicken out of plastic bag, reserving marinade. Spray large skillet with cooking spray. Brown chicken lightly in skillet; add reserved marinade, and about 1 teaspoon of cornstarch or flour to thicken. Cook just until chicken is tender and marinade is warmed. Makes 8 servings of ½ breast each. Serve over steamed brown rice, and add a green vegetable and rolls for a hearty meal.

Nutritional analysis per serving: Cal 142; Fat 3.1g; Chol 71mg; Sod 30mg

Note: It is best to marinate the chicken overnight, but for 3 hours at least before cooking.

The Best of Heart-y Cooking

Minute Chicken

3–4 pounds chicken
3 tablespoons flour
2 cloves garlic, crushed
¼ teaspoon pepper
1 teaspoon sugar
¼ cup hoisin sauce
½ cup chopped green onions

½ cup chopped Chinese
  parsley
2 tablespoons wine
1 (1-inch) piece ginger, crushed
2 tablespoons oyster sauce
¼ cup oil

Chop chicken in bite-size pieces. Marinate chicken in mixture of flour, garlic, pepper, sugar, hoisin sauce, green onions, parsley, wine, ginger, and oyster sauce. Heat oil in large skillet until sizzling hot. Add chicken and quickly stir at highest heat until brown. Lower heat and cook 10 minutes.

Favorite Island Cookery Book I

Chicken with Hoisin Sauce

MARINADE:
2 tablespoons sherry
1½ tablespoons cornstarch
1 tablespoon shoyu

1 clove garlic, grated
½ teaspoon salt

Mix all ingredients well.

1 fryer, cut in bite-size pieces
3 tablespoons oil
2 teaspoons sesame oil

1 piece ginger, mashed
2–3 tablespoons hoisin sauce
Green onion, chopped

Marinate chicken for 10 minutes. Heat oils in large skillet. Add ginger and marinated chicken, and cook. If chicken sticks, add some water. Cover. Cook until tender. Do not overcook. Add hoisin sauce. Garnish with green onion. Serve on bed of boiled broccoli, won bok (Chinese cabbage), and watercress. Yields 3–4 servings.

Favorite Island Cookery Book III

Huli Huli Chicken

This aromatic chicken turned (huli huli) on the spit is a staple at beach picnics, roadside stands, and at fundraisers.

SAUCE:

¼ cup catsup
¼ cup shoyu
½ cup chicken broth
⅓ cup sherry
½ cup fresh lime juice
¼ cup frozen pineapple
  juice concentrate

½ cup brown sugar
1 tablespoon crushed fresh
  ginger
1 clove garlic, crushed
1 teaspoon Worcestershire
  sauce

Mix Sauce ingredients in bowl.

3 chicken fryers, halved
  or quartered

Hawaiian sea salt and pepper
  to taste

Thread chicken onto rotisserie spit. Use clean 1½-inch paintbrush to coat Sauce over cleaned chicken pieces, then sprinkle with salt and pepper. Grill on rotisserie, turning and basting frequently with Sauce until done, 45–60 minutes.

For grilling, place on rack over coals, turning and basting for about 45 minutes. Or roast in 325° preheated oven, basting frequently, for 90 minutes. Serves 6.

Kona on My Plate

Mochiko Chicken

3 pounds chicken, cut in
  pieces and deboned
  (thighs are good)
4 tablespoons mochiko
4 tablespoons cornstarch
4 tablespoons sugar

5 tablespoons shoyu
2 beaten eggs
¼ cup chopped green onions
2 cloves garlic, minced
½ teaspoon salt and
  ajinomoto (MSG)

Soak chicken in remaining ingredients at least 5 hours or overnight. Fry in skillet with a little oil.

The Friends of 'Iolani Palace Cookbook

Chicken Long Rice

1 (3-pound) chicken
Water
1 (½-inch) slice ginger,
  crushed
1 (1¾-ounce) bundle long rice
  (bean threads), soaked in
  water to soften

Salt to taste
3 stalks green onions, chopped

Place chicken in a large pot and cover with water. Add ginger and bring to a boil; lower heat and simmer about 45 minutes to an hour, or until meat falls away from the bones. Remove chicken from broth and discard bones. Return chicken to the broth and add long rice. Simmer until about half the broth is absorbed by the long rice. Season with salt and add green onions just before serving. Serves 4–6.

Note: Although this dish is not "native Hawaiian," it is frequently served at modern Hawaiian lū'aus. To make the dish lower in fat, after chicken is cooked, refrigerate the broth overnight, or until the fat can be skimmed off the top.

Ethnic Foods of Hawai'i

Chicken Waikiki

2–3 pounds chicken pieces
Flour
Salt and pepper to taste
1 (20-ounce) can sliced
  pineapple, or about 2 cups
  fresh pineapple chunks

1 large green pepper, cut
  crosswise (in circles)

Shake the chicken in a paper bag with flour, salt and pepper. Brown in a skillet, then place uncovered in glass baking dish. Bake in 350° oven for 1–1¼ hours. While chicken is baking, make the Sauce. Place pineapple and green pepper over chicken during last half hour of baking time. Serve with rice and a tossed salad or cooked vegetables.

SAUCE:

½ cup sugar
2 tablespoons cornstarch
⅜ cup cider vinegar
⅜ cup pineapple juice

1 tablespoon soy sauce
½ teaspoon ginger
1 chicken bouillon cube

Combine ingredients in a saucepan; cook, stirring constantly and boil 2 minutes until Sauce thickens. Pour immediately over chicken while it is baking.

Friends and Celebrities Cookbook II

"Wai" means water and "kiki" means to spurt, thus Waikiki translates as "spurting water."

Chicken Spareribs

Flour
2–3 pounds chicken wings
   or drumettes
¼ cup oil
1 cup water
¼ cup vinegar

¾ cup brown sugar
3 teaspoons salt
4 tablespoons shoyu
1 slice ginger
3 cloves garlic, crushed

Lightly flour chicken; brown in oil in saucepan. Drain oil and add remaining ingredients to saucepan; simmer for one hour, turning wings occasionally.

Classic Cookbook Recipes

Mandarin Chicken Wings

2 pounds chicken wings
2 eggs, beaten
1 cup cornstarch

1 clove garlic, minced
½ teaspoon salt
½ teaspoon ajinomoto (MSG)

Dip chicken wings in beaten eggs; shake in combination of cornstarch, garlic, salt, and ajinomoto. Deep-fry until golden brown. Pour Sauce over and bake for 30 minutes at 350°.

SAUCE:
⅓ cup sugar
¼ cup water
¼ cup vinegar

2 teaspoons shoyu
Ajinomoto (MSG)
2 tablespoons catsup

Combine Sauce ingredients and pour over chicken wings. Bake for 30 minutes.

A Lei of Recipes

There's fog and there's smog . . . but have you ever heard of vog? Actually, vog is the volcanic fog that occurs when a volcano erupts.

Golden Marinade Chicken on Sticks

½ cup soy sauce
½ cup gin (or sherry)
¼ cup honey
½ teaspoon black pepper
1 teaspoon grated gingerroot

1 clove garlic, grated
About a pound of boneless chicken
1 can large button mushrooms
Barbecue bamboo sticks

Combine first 6 ingredients and set aside. Cut chicken into small pieces that would hold on sticks, then marinate in sauce for at least half an hour. Place chicken pieces on sticks (that have been soaked in water) with mushrooms in between. Broil.

Cook 'em Up Kaua'i

Macadamia Stuffed Chicken Breasts

4 large chicken breasts
¼ cup coarsely chopped macadamia nuts
2 tablespoons finely chopped celery
1 teaspoon finely chopped onion

1 tablespoon soft butter
⅛ teaspoon salt and pepper
1 whole egg, slightly beaten
¼ cup flour, seasoned with salt and pepper
4 tablespoons butter

Bone and skin breasts and flatten with cleaver. Mix nuts, celery, onion, butter, salt and pepper. Slice chicken breasts in half. Put ¼ of the mixture on each breast, and roll up, turning in ends to secure filling. Pin with skewers. Dip into egg and then flour. Fry until brown and done in a medium-hot skillet.

Joys of Hawaiian Cooking

Chicken and Pineapple Curry

The chicken and pineapple are curried together. The result is a mild, yellow curry. Raw, not roasted, spices are used in the curry to add fragrance without altering the desired yellow color. Serve this curry with hot rice.

1½ pounds skinless, boneless
   chicken breasts
2 tablespoons olive oil
2 yellow onions, peeled and
   minced fine
2 teaspoons minced garlic
2 teaspoons minced ginger
1 teaspoon ground coriander
1 teaspoon ground turmeric
½ teaspoon cayenne pepper
⅛ teaspoon ground cinnamon

⅛ teaspoon ground cloves
⅛ teaspoon ground nutmeg
¼ cup water
Fresh lemon juice
Salt to taste
1 cup diced pineapple
½ cup coconut milk
½ cup unsalted, roasted
   cashew nuts
½ cup chopped Chinese
   parsley

Cut chicken into 1-inch squares. Heat oil and sauté onion on low heat, about 10 minutes or until golden. Add garlic, ginger, and spices, and cook 3–4 minutes. Stir chicken in with the spices. Add water and season with lemon juice and salt to taste. Cover and simmer on very low heat for 6–7 minutes. Stir in pineapple and simmer 3–4 minutes. Stir in coconut milk and sprinkle in cashew nuts and Chinese parsley. Cook for one minute and remove from heat. Serve hot with rice. Makes 4 servings.

Burst of Flavor

Chinese Style Roast Chicken

1 (3-pound) fryer

SAUCE:

4 cups water	1 cup soy sauce
3 stalks green onions, chopped	1 tablespoon sugar
4 gingerroot, sliced	1 teaspoon salt
½ cup sherry	

Wash and drain chicken. In a large pot, bring Sauce ingredients to a boil. Place chicken in boiling Sauce; cover and simmer for 30 minutes. Remove chicken and place on rack in roasting pan. Roast in 325° oven for 30–45 minutes or until chicken is brown. Serve hot Sauce separately for dipping chicken. Yields 4 servings.

Favorite Island Cookery Book IV

Hundreds of motion pictures have been filmed in Hawaii since 1913, including top grossing films—*From Here to Eternity, Jurassic Park, Raiders of the Lost Ark, Godzilla, Dinosaur, The Descendants*—generating billions in gross receipts and numerous Academy Award nominations and Oscars. Many television series were also filmed here, including *Hawaii Five-O, Magnum P.I, Gilligan's Island, Fantasy Island, Lost*, etc., and countless episodes and scenes of other shows. The sheer beauty and variety of nature—ocean, beeches, mountains, greenery, flowers, waterfalls—along with near perfect weather make it a sought-after location for film making.

Curried Pineapple-Mango Chicken

Elements such as raisins, mango chutney, and pineapple would normally be served as condiments to top a curry dish; here, they're cooked along with the chicken and spices.

3 skinless, boneless chicken breasts
4 teaspoons sunflower oil, divided
1 cup sliced onion
2 tablespoons peeled and minced ginger
2 tablespoons curry powder
1 teaspoon cinnamon
⅓ cup raisins
3 tablespoons mango chutney
½ cup orange juice
2 cups fresh pineapple chunks
Salt and pepper to taste

Slice chicken into ½-inch-thick strips and place in a small bowl. Toss with 2 teaspoons sunflower oil. Heat skillet to hot and sear chicken for about 30–45 seconds on each side (until pink is just gone). Remove to a plate.

Add remaining oil and sauté onion and ginger together over medium heat until onions are translucent and caramelized. Add curry powder, cinnamon, raisins, mango chutney, orange juice, pineapple chunks, and seasoning to taste, and heat until it just reaches a boil. Return chicken to sauce, stir, and cover for about 2 minutes. Serve over rice or a grain dish like barley. Serves 4.

Hawai'i's Favorite Pineapple Recipes

Seafood

O'ahu's North Shore, where waves can top 30 feet, is popular for its out-standing surfing conditions. Since 1971, O'ahu has been the site of the Triple Crown of Surfing, the longest-running professional surfing competition in the world.

Island Scampi

Scallops or white fish like mahimahi may be substituted for scampi in this recipe.

Flour
6–8 ounces scampi
½ stick butter or margarine
⅓ teaspoon salt
½ ounce white wine
1 teaspoon grated Parmesan
  cheese

⅓ teaspoon chopped fresh
  parsley
2 medium cloves garlic,
  chopped fine

Flour scampi lightly. In saucepan melt butter; sauté scampi, adding salt, wine, Parmesan cheese, parsley, and garlic. Do not overcook.

Classic Cookbook Recipes

It had taken her a month of steady weaving to finish the part she was sitting on, and it would take another several weeks to entirely finish the mat. Demonstrations of Polynesian cultures are both informative and entertaining when talking to the natives at the Polynesian Cultural Center on O'ahu's North Shore.

Shrimp Molokai

2 pounds raw shrimp
1 cup pineapple juice
1 cup sherry
3 tablespoons lemon juice
1 clove garlic, crushed

6 peppercorns
1 whole bay leaf
Hot pepper sauce to taste
1 stick (¼ pound) butter, melted
Sesame seeds

Shell and devein shrimp. Place in a bowl together with a mixture of all the ingredients except the butter and sesame seeds. Marinate for 2–3 hours.

Strain shrimp and brush with melted butter. Roll shrimp in sesame seeds and cook lightly in a buttered pan until they turn pink. Boil remaining marinade liquid for 10 minutes to reduce it, then strain and use as a dip for the shrimp.

Joys of Hawaiian Cooking

Aiea Shrimps with Basil Butter

On the porch of our friend's condo in the hills overlooking Pearl Harbor, there is a huge pot of basil. I was amazed at the large size and fullness of the plant. It seems basil thrives in the Honolulu climate. We sat drinking wine as we watched the sunset over the Pacific, and then were served this superb basil-flavored shrimp.

4 tablespoons butter, room
  temperature
1 tablespoon finely cut basil
Juice of one medium lemon
1 teaspoon chopped parsley

2 tablespoons olive oil
1 pound large, raw shrimp,
  peeled and deveined
Salt and pepper to taste

In a bowl, blend the butter, basil, lemon juice, and parsley. Heat the olive oil in a frying pan. Over medium heat, cook the shrimp just until pink. Add the butter mixture and stir to combine flavors. Add salt and pepper to taste. Garnish with a few sprigs of fresh basil. This will make 2 generous servings.

Honolulu Hawaii Cooking

Party Shrimp Curry

Honolulu parties often have curry as a main dish. Pale pink shrimp in a coconut-accented sauce, surrounded with pretty bowls of condiments, is impressive. The host or hostess can prepare the dinner ahead of time and with only a few last-minute touches, it will be ready for guests.

6 tablespoons butter (⅓ cup)
1 medium-size onion, finely chopped
⅓ cup flour
2 tablespoons grated fresh ginger, or 1 tablespoon dry ginger
2–3 tablespoons curry powder

2 cups milk
1 cup canned or fresh coconut milk
1 pound medium, raw shrimp, peeled and deveined
Salt to taste
Dash of cayenne pepper (optional)

Melt butter in large saucepan. Cook onion just until limp (do not brown). Add flour, ginger, and curry. Stir over a low flame to blend. Gradually add regular and coconut milk, stirring until the mixture is smooth. Add shrimp, with salt to taste, and the cayenne, if used. Cook over a low flame just until shrimp turn pink. This will take about 5 minutes. At this point the curry may be refrigerated until party time.

The condiments for the curry might include chopped peanuts or macadamia nuts, minced green onions, finely diced cucumbers, chutneys, and grated coconut. Curry is served with plenty of hot steamed rice. A dish of sliced fresh tropical fruits is often added to the festive table. Individual portions of curry may be served in papaya shells. This will serve 4, and can be increased for large parties.

Honolulu Hawaii Cooking

 Hawai'i's importance to the United States grew as the U.S. Navy established a huge military base at Pearl Harbor. The Japanese attack on Pearl Harbor on December 7, 1941, was the pivotal event that persuaded the United States to enter World War II. During the war, the port became a strategic naval base and a staging area for U.S. forces in the Pacific. Pearl Harbor is Hawai'i's largest harbor and the nation's only naval base designated as a National Historic Landmark.

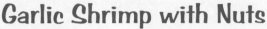

Garlic Shrimp with Nuts

2 tablespoons olive oil
3 cloves garlic, minced
¼ cup chopped scallions
  (white and green parts)
½ cup chopped nuts
  (macadamias or cashews)
1 tablespoon Worcestershire
  sauce

Dash of bottled hot sauce
Dash of cayenne pepper
½ cup dry white wine, or
  vermouth
24 large or jumbo shrimp,
  shelled and deveined

Heat olive oil in a skillet or wok over medium heat. Add garlic, scallions, nuts, Worcestershire, hot sauce, and cayenne pepper. Sauté for 1 or 2 minutes. Add wine and shrimp, and cook just until shrimp are done (pink). Serves 4.

Fresh Catch of the Day...from the Fishwife

Crisp Fried Shrimp

1 pound shrimp or prawns

Remove shells but retain tails. Set aside.

¼ cup mochiko
2 tablespoons cornstarch
½ teaspoon sugar or honey
3 cloves garlic, chopped fine
1 tablespoon finely chopped
  Chinese parsley
1 stalk lemon grass, chopped
  fine, or 1 tablespoon
  lemon zest

1 teaspoon seeded and finely
  chopped red chile peppers
1 teaspoon shoyu
1 teaspoon fish sauce, or ½
  teaspoon salt
1 egg
¼ teaspoon black pepper
¼ cup cold water

Combine all ingredients except cold water; blend well. Stir in cold water and mix well. Preheat enough oil for deep-frying on medium heat. Coat shrimp with mochiko mixture. Deep-fry until golden brown. Drain on paper towels.

Hawai'i's Best Mochi Recipes

Shrimp Shack's "Pan Fried Shrimp"

1 gallon water
¼ cup garlic powder
¹⁄₁₆ cup cayenne powder
4 pounds shell-on black tiger
  shrimp

½ cup margarine to cook and
  dip in
5 tablespoons chopped fresh
  garlic
Rice

Bring water to a boil; add garlic powder and cayenne to water. Drop in shrimp; return to a boil; drain. In sauté pan, heat margarine and chopped garlic. Sauté shrimp till golden brown, serve with rice, garlic butter, and cocktail sauce.

Shrimp Shack
(in Punaluʻu, Oʻahu)

On the drive up the North Shore on Oʻahu (in Punaluʻu), you can't miss the bright yellow Shrimp Shack truck. Irene serves up delicious pan-fried shrimp herself, delivering it personally to you on her umbrella-topped picnic tables. A big sign says, "Suck, peel, dip, eat," and, believe me, you will not need encouragement to do so. Her recipe has been written up in magazines, and she has been featured on the Food and Travel channels. I asked her if she would share her recipe, and she sweetly agreed. We all thank you, Irene. Barney and I licked our fingers and ordered more.

Colorful Stir-Fry

SAUCE:

2 mangoes, peeled and sliced
2 tablespoons frozen orange
concentrate
2 tablespoons frozen apple
concentrate
1 cup chicken broth mixed
with 1 tablespoon cornstarch

2 cloves garlic, minced
¼ teaspoon curry powder
1 teaspoon grated ginger
1 teaspoon chili powder
1 teaspoon cumin seeds

Mix all ingredients in a saucepan and heat until just boiling and thickened.

1 pound large shrimp or
chicken pieces (skin and
fat removed)
Garlic powder
Paprika
Cayenne pepper
1 teaspoon peanut oil

¾ cup sliced onion
4 or 5 fresh mushrooms, sliced
1 large red bell pepper, cored,
seeded, and sliced
¼ cup ground unsalted
macadamia nuts
Hot cooked rice

Season shrimp (or chicken) with garlic powder, paprika, and cayenne pepper to taste. Marinate shrimp or chicken in Sauce in the refrigerator at least one hour.

Heat wok and add peanut oil. Add onion slices and mushrooms and sauté until tender. Remove shrimp or chicken from marinade and add to wok along with the red pepper slices. Stir and cook 1 or 2 minutes. Sprinkle with ground macadamia nuts and serve over hot rice.

Tropical Taste

Each island has its own official color: Ni'ihau, white; Kaua'i, red; O'ahu, yellow; Moloka'i, green; Lana'i, orange; Kaho'olawe, gray; Maui, pink; Hawai'i, red.

Grilled Shrimp with Mango Dipping Sauce

Skewered, coconut-marinated shrimp with lots of taste nuances. Terrific.

1 (14-ounce) can unsweetened coconut milk	1 pound large shrimp, shelled with tail intact
1 tablespoon minced garlic	Wooden skewers, soaked
3 Hawaiian chili peppers, minced	overnight
Zest of 1 lime, grated	Salt and cracked pepper to taste
½ teaspoon paprika	¼ cup vegetable oil

In medium bowl, whisk together coconut milk, garlic, chili, zest, and paprika. Add shrimp and marinate overnight in refrigerator. Also soak wooden skewers overnight.

Heat grill. Drain shrimp and season with salt and pepper. Add vegetable oil and toss lightly until coated. Thread soaked skewers with 4 shrimp. Grill 1½ minutes on both sides or until shrimp are opaque. Serve with Mango Dipping Sauce. Makes 4–5 main-course servings.

MANGO DIPPING SAUCE:

1 cup red wine vinegar	½ red bell pepper, small dice
½ cup sugar	½ green bell pepper, small dice
½ mango, puréed	
1 lime, juiced	

In medium saucepan, bring vinegar and sugar to a boil, then lower heat to medium and cook until syrupy consistency. When cooled, combine in blender with mango purée and lime juice. Stir in diced peppers. Reserve.

Kona on My Plate

The production of sugar was first introduced in the early 1800s on Kaua'i. By 1877, there were eight plantations on Kaua'i, and over the years a total of 32 plantations operated at one time or another. By 2001, only two plantations were left in the state, one in Kaua'i, and one in Maui.

Baked Mahi

8 mahimahi fillets	8 dill sprigs
8 tablespoons mayonnaise	Black pepper
8 tablespoons lime juice	Lime wedges

Pat fillets dry. Place in aluminum foil, smear top with mayonnaise and dribble over with lime juice. Add sprigs of dill and sprinkle with pepper before sealing the edges of foil. Bake in preheated 350° oven for 20 minutes. Unwrap; garnish with lime wedges. Serves 6–8.

Favorite Island Cookery Book V

Spicy Blackened Mahi

Use spices according to your own taste, and serve with rice or potatoes and a green salad.

1 pound fresh mahi fillets	Garlic powder
(4 pieces, may substitute	Cayenne pepper
any mild fish)	White pepper
Sweet paprika	Black pepper
Salt (optional)	Oregano
Onion powder	Dried thyme

Season fish by sprinkling spices on one by one and pressing into fish. Let stand in refrigerator to absorb spices for about one hour.

Preheat cast-iron skillet to high heat and sear fish on both sides. Turn down heat and cook for about 5–8 minutes or until fish is done. Makes 4 servings.

Nutritional analysis per serving: Cal 132; Fat 1.73g; Chol 77mg; Sod 252mg

The Best of Heart-y Cooking

Peppered 'Ahi
with Dijon-Wasabi Sauce

2 tablespoons freshly cracked   ½ teaspoon chili powder
  black peppercorns   1 (2x6-inch) 'ahi block
½ teaspoon paprika

Heat skillet until very hot. In a pie plate, combine pepper, paprika, and chili powder; coat 'ahi block and sear in hot pan on all
sides, about one minute. Reserve.

DIJON-WASABI SAUCE:

1 teaspoon minced fresh   1 tablespoon mirin sake
  ginger   1 tablespoon brown sugar
1 clove garlic, minced   1 tablespoon wasabi paste,
2 tablespoons soy sauce   to taste
¼ cup Dijon mustard   Sesame seed oil

In the same skillet over medium heat, add ginger, garlic, soy
sauce, mustard, mirin sake, and sugar; heat until sugar dissolves. Add wasabi paste and sesame seed oil to taste. Spoon
sauce onto serving platter; top with sliced 'ahi. Serves 2.

Dd's Table Talk

Each year hundreds of the North Pacific 30- to 40-ton endangered hump-
back whales migrate to the main Hawaiian Islands during the months of
November through May. The round-trip distance is approximately 6,000
miles, one of the longest migration distances of any animal species. While in
Hawai'i, they do not feed, but rely upon stored energy. The humpbacks have
become renowned for their various acrobatic displays.

Steamed 'Ōpakapaka with Shiitake Mushroom and Butter Shoyu

4 (6-ounce) 'ōpakapaka fillets
   (pink snapper)
¼ cup oil
3 tablespoons soy sauce,
   divided
1 teaspoon minced ginger

2 tablespoons butter
2 cups sliced fresh shiitake
   mushrooms
¼ cup chopped cilantro
Salt and pepper to taste
Fresh ti leaves

Marinate 'ōpakapaka fillets for one hour in a combination of oil, 2 tablespoons soy sauce and ginger.

Steam fillets 8–10 minutes, or until fish flakes easily when tested with a fork. Set fish aside on a heated platter.

Melt butter in a heavy skillet; add shiitake mushrooms, and sauté until mushrooms are just limp. Add remaining 1 tablespoon soy sauce and cilantro. Season to taste with salt and pepper. Pour shiitake mushroom mixture over fillets. Serves 4.

LUALUA METHOD:

Take 2 ti leaves, and lay them across each other. Place 1 'ōpakapaka fillet in the middle, top with shiitake mushrooms, and pour 1 tablespoon of the butter sauce on it; top with cilantro. Tie ti leaves together to form a basket. Steam 8–10 minutes.

Recipe by Chef Sam Choy, Sam Choy Restaurants of Hawai'i
Fresh Catch of the Day...from the Fishwife

Opah Curry Kabobs

2 pounds opah fillets
  (moonfish)
¼ cup oil
2 tablespoons lemon juice
2 tablespoons grated or
  minced onion

¼ teaspoon dried mustard
1 teaspoon curry powder
Salt and pepper to taste
½ teaspoon dried thyme
Onion chunks, mushrooms, and
  zucchini wheels

Cut fillets into bite-sized pieces, and place in a nonaluminum bowl or dish. Combine oil, lemon juice, onion, dried mustard, curry powder, salt and pepper, and thyme and pour over fish. Marinate fish for one hour. Stir mixture a few times during marinating process.

When ready to cook, thread fish pieces, onion chunks, mushrooms, and zucchini wheels on skewers. Cook 4 inches from coals. Baste fish pieces often with marinade, and turn kabobs once while cooking. Serves 4.

Fresh Catch of the Day...from the Fishwife

Shoyu Butterfish

1 cup shoyu
1 cup water
½ cup sugar
2 cloves garlic, crushed

1 slice ginger
2 butterfish fillets, rinsed in
  warm water
Hot rice

In large pan with cover, add all ingredients, except fish; bring to a boil. Add fish. Reduce heat and simmer until fish flakes. Serve with rice.

Note: Butterfish has a tender texture and a rich, sweet flavor. In some regions they are called dollarfish, Pacific pompano, or pomfret.

Classic Cookbook Recipes

Casian-Spiced Taape with Papaya Relish

Casian is Chef Elmer Guzman's version of blackened fish—a blend of Cajun and Asian. Taape can withstand the bold spices and goes very well with the refreshing papaya relish.

4–6 (6-ounces each) whole taape (blue-striped snapper), scaled and gutted	Chef E Spice to taste (see recipe below) 6 tablespoons oil

Season fish moderately with Chef E Spice. Heat oil in sauté pan over medium heat. Cook fish 3–4 minutes on each side until done. Serve with Papaya Relish. Serves 4–6.

PAPAYA RELISH:

1 whole ripe papaya, skinned, seeded, and diced	Juice from ½ lime 2 tablespoons oil
½ cup diced red onions	Salt and pepper to taste
¼ cup sliced green onions	

Combine all ingredients and chill. Recommended wine: Pino Grigio.

The Shoreline Chef

Chef E Spice

6½ cups iodized salt	1½ cups onion powder
3¼ cups paprika	4 cups dried oregano
½ cup cayenne	4 cups dried thyme
2½ cups ground black pepper	¾ cup togarashi (Japanese seasoning)
2½ cups granulated garlic	

Combine all ingredients. Keeps well in tightly sealed jars.

The Shoreline Chef

On O'ahu, at Hanauma Bay's Toilet Bowl you can find out what it might be like to be flushed down a toilet—that is, if the conditions are right. The Toilet Bowl is a circular rock formation where waves "flush" in and out of an opening. The pool of water rises and falls with the tide, simulating the flushing of a toilet.

Baked Snapper with Ginger Salsa

Fresh 'ōpakapaka (snapper) from Kona waters is the star of this easy, succulent dish.

GINGER SALSA:

3 medium tomatoes, peeled and diced

2 tablespoons chopped scallions

2 tablespoons chopped fresh cilantro

2 tablespoons diced jícama

3 tablespoons fresh lime juice, divided

2–3 teaspoons minced Hawaiian chili pepper

2 teaspoons peeled and minced fresh ginger

Combine tomatoes, scallions, cilantro, jícama, 2 tablespoons lime juice, chili pepper, and ginger in bowl. Cover and let sit for at least one hour.

4 (6-ounce) fresh red snapper fillets

1 cup dry white wine

Preheat oven to 425°. Place snapper fillets in a shallow pan and cover with wine and remaining one tablespoon lime juice. Cover pan with aluminum foil and bake for 25 minutes or until fish flakes easily with a fork. Arrange fish on serving plate and spoon Ginger Salsa on top. Serves 4.

Kona on My Plate

Quite a mouthful, Hawai'i's state fish, the humuhumu nukunuku a pua'a, is pronounced hoo-moo-hoo-moo noo-koo-noo-koo ahh poo-ah-ah.

Kaua'i Fillet of Sole

4 fish fillets (about 1 pound)
Salt and pepper
2 tablespoons lime juice,
  divided
Flour for dredging
3 or 4 tablespoons butter

¼ cup heavy cream
1 avocado, peeled, and sliced
¼ cup coarsely chopped
  macadamia nuts
Lime wedges

Sprinkle fish with salt and pepper and 1 tablespoon lime juice; let stand 10 minutes. Dredge with flour. Sauté in butter 1–3 minutes on each side until nicely browned. Remove to warm platter, sprinkle with remaining lime juice. Keep warm.

To the pan, add cream and bring to rapid boil, scraping brown particles free; spoon over fish. Top with avocado slices, macadamia nuts, and lime wedges. Serves 2.

Cook 'em Up Kaua'i

Gwen and Barney take a hikers' break at one of the memorable overlooks, where rainbows of colors dance along the canyon peaks of Waimea Canyon in Kaua'i. Dubbed by Mark Twain, the "Grand Canyon of the Pacific," it is ten miles long and about 3,600 feet deep.

Imitation Crab Patties with Thai Chili Sauce

1 pound imitation crab,
  coarsely chopped
1 cup bread crumbs
2 eggs
1 clove garlic, minced
½ cup minced onion
2 stalks green onions, chopped

Vegetable oil
1 red bell pepper, seeded and
  chopped
¼ cup mayonnaise
2 ounces cream cheese,
  softened
Salt and white pepper

In a mixing bowl, combine crab, bread crumbs, and eggs. Reserve. In a skillet over medium-high heat, sauté garlic and onions in oil. Add bell pepper and sauté until tender. Remove from heat and cool. Add with remaining ingredients to reserved crab mixture, blending well, seasoning with salt and pepper. Cover and refrigerate for one hour.

Form crab mixture into patties and fry until golden brown. Drain on paper towels. Serve with Thai Chili Sauce. Serves 4.

THAI CHILI SAUCE:

1 cup sugar
½ cup water
½ cup rice wine vinegar
1 clove garlic, minced

1 teaspoon salt
1 tablespoon garlic chili paste
2 teaspoons chopped fresh
  cilantro

In a small saucepan, combine all ingredients; simmer until syrupy; cool. Stir in cilantro. Set aside. Makes 1½ cups.

Variation: Form mixture into 1-inch balls. Combine 1 egg and ¼ cup milk. Dip crab balls into egg wash. Wrap with shredded won ton pi, pressing firmly. Deep-fry until golden brown. Drain on paper towels; serve with your favorite sauce.

Dd's Table Talk

Cakes

As part of performances, these natives adeptly climb these 40-foot coconut trees showing remarkable strength and ability. If you really want some fresh coconuts . . .

Banana-Pineapple Upside-Down Cake

⅜ cup butter, softened
¾ cup sugar
1 egg
2 cups flour
2 teaspoons baking powder
½ teaspoon salt
¾ cup milk

1 banana, mashed
⅓ cup butter
⅔ cup brown sugar
1 cup crushed pineapple, drained
½ cup chopped nuts

Cream ⅜ cup butter and sugar; add beaten egg. Sift flour, baking powder, and salt; add gradually with milk to butter mixture. Fold in mashed banana. Melt ⅓ cup butter in 8-inch-square pan or small tube pan. Sprinkle brown sugar over butter; add well-drained crushed pineapple and chopped nuts. Pour batter over this mixture and bake in 350° preheated oven for 25–30 minutes. Serves 6–8.

Cook 'em Up Kaua'i

Mango Upside-Down Cake

2 tablespoons lemon juice
2 cups sliced, ripe mangoes
1 tablespoon margarine
⅓ cup packed brown sugar
¼ cup oil
¾ cup sugar

1 egg, well beaten
1¼ cups flour
2 teaspoons baking powder
¼ teaspoon salt
½ cup milk

Sprinkle lemon juice over sliced mangoes. Melt margarine in an 8-inch cake pan. Sprinkle brown sugar evenly over the margarine. Place mangoes on top of brown sugar. In a mixing bowl, cream oil and sugar thoroughly. Add egg and mix again. Sift dry ingredients and add alternately with milk. Pour batter over mangoes. Bake about 1 hour in a 375° oven. When cake is done, remove from oven and turn it upside-down. Serve warm.

Variation: Bake in muffin tins for individual servings. Serve with whipped cream.

Joys of Hawaiian Cooking

Butter Cake

1 cup butter, softened	1 teaspoon salt
1¾ cups sugar	1 teaspoon baking soda
4 eggs, separated	1 cup milk
3 cups flour	2 teaspoons cream of tartar

Cream together butter and sugar. Add egg yolks. Sift together flour, salt, and baking soda. Add alternately with milk. Beat egg whites, add cream of tartar, and beat until frothy. Fold into batter. Pour into greased 9x13-inch pan or Bundt pan. Bake in 350° oven for 25–30 minutes.

A Lei of Recipes

Coconut Broiled Oatmeal Cake

1½ cups boiling water	1½ cups all-purpose flour
1 cup old-fashioned oats	1 teaspoon baking powder
½ cup butter, softened	1 teaspoon baking soda
1 cup sugar	1 teaspoon cinnamon
1 cup firmly packed brown	½ teaspoon ground ginger
sugar	½ teaspoon salt
2 large eggs	¼ teaspoon allspice
1 teaspoon vanilla extract	¼ teaspoon nutmeg

Preheat oven to 350°; lightly grease a 9x13-inch baking pan. In a mixing bowl, combine water and oats; let stand 15 minutes. In a mixing bowl, cream together butter and sugars. Add eggs and extract. Stir in oats and remaining ingredients. Pour mixture into prepared pan; bake 30–35 minutes. Serves 12.

FROSTING:

½ cup butter, melted	6 tablespoons cream
1 cup firmly packed brown	1 cup chopped walnuts
sugar	1 cup flaked coconut

In a mixing bowl, combine ingredients. Spread onto hot cake. Place under broiler until bubbly.

Dd's Table Talk II

Pumpkin Pie Cake

1 (29-ounce) can pumpkin
1 (13-ounce) can evaporated
  milk
3 eggs, beaten
1¼ cups sugar
2 teaspoons cinnamon
1 teaspoon nutmeg
½ teaspoon salt
½ teaspoon ginger
½ teaspoon cloves
1 (18¼-ounce) box yellow
  cake mix
1 cup chopped walnuts
1 cup butter, melted

Combine all ingredients except cake mix, nuts, and butter. Pour into greased, 9x13-inch pan. Sprinkle dry cake mix over pumpkin mixture. Pat down gently with spoon. Sprinkle with chopped nuts. Drizzle melted butter over cake. Bake 50–60 minutes in 350° oven.

Favorite Island Cookery Book III

'Ono Coconut Cake

3 cups cake flour
1½ cups sugar
5 teaspoons baking powder
½ teaspoon salt
8 egg whites
1½ cups fresh coconut milk
  (if not available, use canned)
1½ cups freshly grated coconut
  (or packaged)

Sift flour, sugar, and baking powder together. Add salt to egg whites and beat until stiff but not too dry. Add coconut milk to dry ingredients and beat till smooth. Fold in coconut and egg whites. Put into 2 (9-inch) cake pans that have been greased and floured. Bake for 40–45 minutes at 350°. Cool.

Frost with white frosting and sprinkle generously with additional freshly grated coconut.

Friends and Celebrities Cookbook II

Coconut milk is not the liquid inside a coconut (but you can drink this "water"). To make coconut milk, grate the flesh of a coconut in a food processor or blender. Add an equal amount of boiling water (or combination of coconut water and water), and blend till liquefied. Strain through a fine strainer.

Coconut Custard Mochi

½ cup butter, softened
3 cups sugar
4 eggs
Water
1 (12-ounce) can coconut milk
1 (13-ounce) can evaporated
  milk

4 cups mochiko (2 [10-ounce]
  packages)
3 teaspoons baking powder
2 teaspoons vanilla
Toasted sesame seeds
  (optional)

Using an electric mixer, beat butter and sugar. Add eggs and beat well. Add water to coconut milk to make 2 cups liquid. Also add water to evaporated milk to make 2 cups liquid. Put all the milk, mochi flour, baking powder, and vanilla into the creamed mixture, and mix well. Pour batter into greased and floured 9x13-inch pan. Sprinkle toasted sesame seeds over batter. Bake at 350° for one hour.

Hawai'i's Best Mochi Recipes

Cocoa Mochi

1 (1-pound) box mochiko
1¾ cups white sugar
3 tablespoons cocoa powder
1 teaspoon baking soda
2 eggs, beaten

1 (12-ounce) can evaporated
  milk
1 can coconut milk
¼ cup butter, melted
1 teaspoon vanilla

Preheat oven to 350°. Grease and flour a 9x13-inch pan. Sift mochiko, sugar, cocoa, and baking soda into a large mixing bowl. Add eggs, milks, butter, and vanilla. Mix until batter is smooth. Pour batter into prepared pan. Bake for 1 hour and 10 minutes. Cool completely and cut with a plastic knife or it will stick.

Unbearably Good! Mochi Lovers' Cookbook

Peach Refrigerator Cake

FILLING:

1 (13-ounce) can evaporated
milk
1 (26-ounce) can sliced
peaches, undrained

½ cup sugar
1 (3-ounce) box orange Jell-O
1 envelope unflavored gelatin

Put can of evaporated milk in freezer. Heat peaches with syrup and sugar and remove from heat. Add Jell-O and mix well. Add gelatin which has been softened in ¼ cup water. Cool. Beat icy cold can of evaporated milk until whipped. Fold into peach mixture gradually.

1 large chiffon cake   **Whipped cream**

Coat a 9x13-inch pan generously with butter. Break cake into bite-size pieces. Put in buttered pan. Layer cake pieces and Filling, starting with cake first. Frost with whipped cream. Chill.

Favorite Island Cookery Book I

Editor's Extra: Good over most any kind of cake.

Michelle Wie was born in Honolulu in 1989 and began playing golf at the age of four. At age seven, she played her first 18-hole round and finished 14-over par. At age 10, she shot a 64, and later became the youngest player to qualify in a USGA amateur championship event. Among her many accomplishments, at age 11, Wie won the Hawaii State Women's Stroke Play Championship, the Jennie K. Wilson Invitational, and reached the third round of match play at the US Women's Amateur Public Links Championship—a tournament she won at age 13. Michelle, who is over six feet tall, has won several professional championships. Here's what Fred Couples says after playing with her: "When you see her hit a golf ball . . . there's nothing that prepares you for it. It's just the scariest thing you've ever seen."

Glazed Sponge Cake

1 cup butter or margarine,
  softened
1½ cups sugar
4 eggs, beaten
1 teaspoon vanilla, lemon,
  or almond extract

2 cups flour, unsifted
½ can pie filling (cherry,
  blueberry, apple, etc.)

Cream butter and sugar till fluffy. Add eggs a little at a time (3 pourings). Add extract. Blend in flour. Spread batter in well-greased 10½x15½x1-inch pan. Score lightly with knife in 24 pieces. Drop a teaspoonful of pie filling in center of each square. Bake at 350° for 30 minutes.

Favorite Island Cookery Book II

Piña Colada Cake

1 (18¼-ounce) package
  yellow cake mix
1 (3¾-ounce) package vanilla
  pudding
1 (15-ounce) can Coco Lopez
  Cream of Coconut, divided
½ cup plus 2 tablespoons
  rum, divided

⅓ cup vegetable oil
4 eggs
1 (8-ounce) can crushed
  pineapple, drained
Whipped cream, pineapple
  chunks, maraschino cherries,
  and toasted coconut for
  garnish

Preheat oven to 350°; well grease and flour a 10-inch Bundt or tube pan. In a large mixing bowl, combine cake mix, pudding mix, ½ cup cream of coconut, ½ cup rum, oil, and eggs. Beat well. Stir in pineapple. Pour into prepared pan; bake for 50–55 minutes. Cool 10 minutes.

With a table knife or skewer, poke holes about 1 inch apart in cake almost to the bottom. Combine remaining cream of coconut and remaining 2 tablespoons rum; slowly spoon over cake. Chill thoroughly. Store in refrigerator. Garnish as desired. Serves 12.

Dd's Table Talk

Paradise Cake

1 cup vegetable shortening
2 cups sugar
4 eggs, beaten
3 bananas, mashed (by hand, not in a processor)
1 ripe mango or papaya, peeled, seeded, and mashed
2 teaspoons salt
1 teaspoon baking soda
3 teaspoons baking powder
4 cups flour
6 tablespoons sour milk or cream
2 tablespoons lemon juice
Grated lemon rind from 1 lemon
2 cups chopped macadamia nuts

Cream shortening and sugar. Add beaten eggs, bananas, and mango or papaya. Sift salt, baking soda, baking powder, and flour, and add to fruit mixture with milk, lemon juice, rind, and nuts. Mix well and turn into a well-greased Bundt pan. Bake at 350° for one hour. Cool in pan.

Note: You may make sour milk by adding one tablespoon lemon juice to regular milk and mixing.

TOPPING:
1 (8-ounce) package cream cheese, room temperature
2 cups whipped cream topping
½ (6-ounce) can unsweetened pineapple juice
1 cup ground macadamia nuts

Mix cream cheese and whipped cream topping. Add pineapple juice slowly until reaching a light consistency, about half the can. Top cooled cake with mixture and sprinkle with nuts. May be made a day ahead.

Hawaii's Best Tropical Food & Drinks

Tropical Cheesecake

Cheesecake is one of the most popular desserts around the world, and Hawaii's abundance of fruits makes it a refreshing end to any meal. This can be made a day ahead, adding the fruit just before serving.

4 (3-ounce) packages cream cheese, room temperature
2 large eggs
1 teaspoon vanilla
½ cup plus 5 tablespoons sugar, divided
Dash cinnamon (optional)

1 (9-inch) graham cracker crust
3 ounces macadamia nuts, ground
1 pint sour cream
Fruit of choice
Apple jelly

Using an electric mixer or whisk, beat cream cheese with eggs until smooth. Add vanilla, ½ cup sugar, and cinnamon, and beat. Cover graham cracker crust with macadamia nuts and top with cream cheese mixture. Bake at 325° for 25 minutes, or until set. Cool. Add 5 tablespoons sugar to sour cream and pour on pie. Bake at 325° for 20 minutes until set. Cool.

Just before serving, top cheesecake in a decorative pattern with your choice of sliced or whole fruit. Melt apple jelly and brush over fruit.

Note: If you are using bananas, brush with lemon juice to prevent discoloration.

Hawaii's Best Tropical Food & Drinks

Panaewa Zoo, located inside a forest reserve on the island of Hawai'i, is the only tropical rainforest zoo in the United States. This 12-acre zoo is home to more than 75 species of animals, birds, and reptiles. Among the rainforest animals are the native Hawaiian gallinule (wading bird from Rallida family), 'io (hawk), and nene (goose).

Liliko'i Cheesecake

CRUST:

1⅔ cups graham cracker
  crumbs (or 22 squares
  finely rolled)

3 tablespoons honey
¼ cup butter or margarine,
  softened

Mix together crumbs, honey, and margarine, and press firmly into a 9-inch springform pan.

CHEESECAKE:

1 envelope or 1 tablespoon
  gelatin (unflavored)
½ cup liliko'i (passion fruit)
  juice, divided

½–¾ cup sugar
½ cup boiling water
2 (8-ounce) packages cream
  cheese, softened

In a large bowl, soften gelatin in a little of the fruit juice; mix in sugar. Add boiling water and remaining liliko'i juice, and stir until gelatin is completely dissolved. With electric mixer, beat in cream cheese until smooth. Pour into Crust; chill until firm (about 2 hours). Makes about 8 servings.

Note: For a sweeter cake, use ¾ cup sugar.

Cook 'em Up Kaua'i

Liliko'i cheesecake is like no other. This was even more delicious than it looks!

Lemon Cheesecake

1 package Pillsbury Lemon
  Cake Mix
3 eggs
1 cup plus 3–4 tablespoons
  sour cream, divided

1 (3-ounce) package cream
  cheese, softened
⅓ cup oil

Preheat oven to 350°. Lightly grease bottom only of 9x13-inch baking pan. In large bowl, blend cake mix (reserving glaze mix from package), eggs, 1 cup sour cream, cream cheese, and oil until moistened. Beat 2 minutes on medium speed (portable mixer can use highest speed). Pour into prepared pan. Bake at 350° for 30–40 minutes or until toothpick inserted in center comes out clean.

Cool cake in pan on cooling rack. Blend glaze mix with remaining sour cream. Drizzle over cooled cake. Refrigerate leftovers.

Classic Cookbook Recipes

Chocolate Chip Cheesecake

Soooooo yummy!

1½ cups graham cracker
  crumbs
⅓ cup Hershey's Cocoa
⅓ cup sugar
⅓ cup butter, melted
3 (8-ounce) packages cream
  cheese, softened

1 (14-ounce) can sweetened
  condensed milk
3 eggs
2 teaspoons vanilla
1 cup mini chocolate chips
  (semisweet), divided
1 teaspoon all-purpose flour

Heat oven to 300°. In bowl, combine cracker crumbs, cocoa, sugar, and butter. Press evenly in bottom of 9-inch springform pan. Beat cream cheese until fluffy. Add sweetened condensed milk; beat until smooth. Add eggs and vanilla. Mix well. Toss ½ chips with flour to coat. Stir into cheese mixture. Pour into pan. Sprinkle remaining chips over top. Bake one hour, then turn oven off and leave cheesecake in one additional hour. Refrigerate until firm.

Seasoned with Aloha Vol. 2

Chocolate Cheesecake

Cheesecake so creamy and chocolatey, you'll want to make it for every occasion!

CRUST:

1 cup chocolate macadamia
   nut cookie crumbs

¼ cup white sugar
¼ cup unsalted butter, melted

Combine and mix well; press mixture into a 9-inch springform pan.

4 squares chocolate, or
   4 ounces semisweet
   chocolate chips
1 (8-ounce) package cream
   cheese, softened
½ cup white sugar
1½ cups sour cream, divided

2 large eggs
1 teaspoon vanilla extract
¼ cup finely diced macadamia
   nuts
2 tablespoons firmly packed
   brown sugar

Melt chocolate in microwave on HIGH and stir; keep warm. Whip cream cheese and white sugar together until creamy. Add ½ cup sour cream and eggs. Blend in 3 ounces of the melted chocolate (reserving some for drizzle) and vanilla. Pour mixture into prepared Crust. Bake at 325° for 35–40 minutes or until cheesecake center is set.

Blend remaining 1 cup sour cream, macadamia nuts, and brown sugar and spread over cheesecake. Bake for 5 more minutes. Cool to room temperature. Drizzle remaining one ounce melted chocolate over cheesecake. Chill for 4 hours. Makes 8 servings.

Sugar and Spice–Cookies Made with Love

Cookies

PHOTO BY JIM STEINHART / WWW.PLANETWARE.COM

This statue of King Kamehameha I stands in front of the Judiciary Building in Honolulu. King Kamehameha I was the first ruler to unite all the Hawaiian Islands under one rule. He was king from 1795 to 1819.

Guava Crispies

¾ cup butter, divided
⅓ cup guava jelly
2 tablespoons lemon juice
2 tablespoons sugar
¼ teaspoon salt
1 egg yolk, slightly beaten
¼ cup chopped macadamia
   nuts

1 cup flour
½ teaspoon salt
½ teaspoon baking soda
½ cup brown sugar
1 cup quick oats

Combine ¼ cup butter, guava jelly, lemon juice, sugar, and salt in the top of a double boiler. Heat until the guava jelly has dissolved. Stir a part of this into slightly beaten yolk, then return the egg mixture to the rest of the jelly mixture. Heat and stir until the mixture thickens. Add nuts. Remove from heat and cool.

Sift flour, salt, and soda over brown sugar and remaining ½ cup butter. Cut together with 2 knives until coarse crumbs form. Add oatmeal and mix well. Pat half of the mixture into the bottom of a 9-inch-square pan. Spread guava mixture on top and sprinkle remaining oatmeal mixture on top. Bake in a 350° oven for 25 minutes. Cool and cut into squares. Makes 3 dozen.

Joys of Hawaiian Cooking

Hawaiian Vowel Pronunciation Guide:

a – Pronounced "ah" and never "ay." Kamehameha, for example, starts off "kah...," not "Kam..." (as in the word camera).

e – Pronounced "ay" as in the long "a" in the English language. Kamehameha, for example, is roughly pronounced "kah may hah may hah."

i – Pronounced "ee" as in the long "e" in the English language. Waikiki, for example, is pronounced "wah ee kee kee." "Wah" and "ee" are slurred to sound like "wye." Try it. Likewise, "kai," as in Hawai'i Kai, is pronounced "kah ee." When slurred, it sounds like "kye."

o – Pronounced "oh," never differently.

u – Pronounced "oo" as in "goo," never differently.

Almond Cookies

3 cups all-purpose flour
1 cup sugar
½ teaspoon salt
½ teaspoon baking soda

1 cup margarine, softened
1 egg, slightly beaten
1 teaspoon almond extract
⅓ cup whole almonds

Preheat oven to 350°. Combine flour, sugar, salt, and baking soda. Add margarine and mix until mixture resembles cornmeal. Add in egg and almond extract. Roll mixture into walnut-size balls. Place a whole almond on each ball, pressing down slightly. Place on greased cookie sheet. Bake for 12–15 minutes or until light brown.

Hawai'i's Favorite Firehouse Recipes

Famous Cookies

2 sticks butter, softened
¾ cup sugar (brown or white)
1 teaspoon baking soda
1 teaspoon water
1 egg
½ teaspoon salt

1 teaspoon vanilla
3 cups flour
½ cup shredded coconut
1 cup chopped nuts
2 cups chocolate chips

Cream butter and sugar. Mix soda with water and add to cream mixture, along with egg, salt, and vanilla. Mix in flour and remaining ingredients. Chill for an hour. Preheat oven to 350°. Drop dough by spoonfuls onto cookie sheet and bake 12 minutes.

Island Flavors

Lemonade Cookies

1 cup butter or margarine,
  softened
1 cup sugar
2 eggs, beaten
3 cups flour

1 teaspoon baking soda
1 (6-ounce) can frozen
  lemonade concentrate,
  thawed, divided
Colored sugar for sprinkling

Cream butter with sugar and well-beaten eggs. Mix flour and baking soda, and add alternately with ½ of the thawed lemonade concentrate to butter mixture.

Drop by teaspoonfuls onto greased cookie sheets. Bake at 375° until slightly brown—about 10 minutes. Remove to rack to cool and brush hot cookies with remaining lemonade concentrate. Sprinkle tops lightly with colored sugars for a decorative effect.

Hilo Woman's Club Cookbook

Banyan trees *(Ficus benghalensis)* prefer areas of high humidity and moist soils. These trees put down multiple root systems. They have a main trunk, but as the branches grow, they too put down roots, and when they touch the ground, they grow deep roots themselves, supporting the branch and nourishing the main trunk. Older, mature banyan trees in Hawai'i can completely fill an acre or two of land, creating natural parks beneath their branches and between their vertical root systems.

Coconut Macadamia Nut Crisps

¾ cup butter, softened
¾ cup sugar
½ cup firmly packed brown
  sugar
1 large egg
1 teaspoon vanilla extract
2 cups all-purpose flour

1 teaspoon baking powder
1 teaspoon baking soda
½ teaspoon salt
1 cup chopped macadamia nuts
1 cup old-fashioned oats
½ cup flaked coconut

Preheat oven to 375°; lightly grease baking sheets. In a mixing bowl, cream together butter and sugars until fluffy. Add egg and extract. Stir in remaining ingredients until well blended. Drop by teaspoonfuls 1 inch apart on prepared sheets. Bake 8–10 minutes until edges are brown. Makes 5 dozen.

Dd's Table Talk II

Fresh Coconut Macaroons

1 fresh coconut (about 1½
  pounds)
4 egg whites

½ cup sugar
¾ teaspoon almond extract

Remove coconut from shell; grate it and measure 3 cups. In a mixing bowl, combine grated coconut, unbeaten egg whites, sugar, and almond extract. Stir until well blended. Drop batter by teaspoons, about 1 inch apart, onto a lightly greased baking sheet or a cookie sheet lined with parchment paper. Lightly press down each cookie with the back of a spoon.

Bake in 325° oven for 25–35 minutes, or until lightly browned. Cool on a wire rack, then store in an airtight container. Yields 2 dozen cookies.

Tropical Taste

White Chocolate Coconut Cookies

These are especially light and heavenly cookies with a distinctively coconut-y flavor.

1 cup butter, softened	½ teaspoon baking soda
1 cup white sugar	1 teaspoon salt
2 large eggs	1 cup shredded coconut
1 teaspoon rum extract or dark rum	1 (12-ounce) package white chocolate chips
3 cups all-purpose flour	

Preheat oven to 350°. Oil baking sheet. Cream together butter and sugar until light. Add eggs and rum extract or rum. Sift together flour, soda, and salt, and gradually mix into egg-butter mixture. Fold in coconut and white chocolate chips.

Drop mounds of dough onto oiled baking sheet. Bake for 35–40 minutes in 350° oven. Remove cookie sheet from oven and let cool.

Variation: Add ½ cup chopped, dried pineapple to coconut mixture for a piña colada cookie.

Sugar and Spice–Cookies Made with Love

Kilauea Lighthouse, located on Kaua'i, is the northernmost point of the main Hawaiian Islands. It has the world's largest clamshell lens, sending a beacon 90 miles out to sea. (Compared to other lenses, a clamshell lens has only two flash panels and sends light beams in only two directions as it rotates.) Built in 1913, the lighthouse was in use until 1976.

Chocolate Macadamia Nut Cookies

1 cup whole macadamia nuts
5 ounces semisweet chocolate
½ cup butter
2 large eggs
½ cup white sugar
1 teaspoon vanilla extract
2 cups all-purpose flour

¾ cup cocoa
1 teaspoon baking soda
1 teaspoon salt
¾ cup semisweet chocolate
  chips
Beaten egg white

Preheat oven to 350°. Oil a baking sheet. Place whole macadamia nuts in another pan and bake in oven for 5–8 minutes or until golden brown; set aside. When cool, chop, reserving ¼ cup for garnish.

Combine chocolate and butter in microwave-proof dish. Melt in microwave 1–2 minutes; cool, then add eggs, sugar, and vanilla. Sift together flour, cocoa, soda, and salt. Mix into egg batter. Fold in macadamia nuts (except ¼ cup for garnish) and semisweet chocolate chips until well blended.

Scoop out spoonfuls of mixture onto oiled baking sheet, about 1 inch apart. Brush with beaten egg white and sprinkle with chopped macadamia nuts. Bake on the middle rack of a 350° oven for 30 minutes or until edges are browned. Remove cookie sheet from oven and let cool. Serve with coffee ice cream. Makes about 3½ dozen.

Sugar and Spice–Cookies Made with Love

Judy's Macadamia Nut Bars

These easy-to-make cookies are some of the most addictively delicious morsels you can imagine. Macadamia nuts give a taste of Hawaiian crunch and flavor. This recipe, from a special family friend, is a winner.

FILLING:

2 eggs
1 teaspoon vanilla
1¼ cups brown sugar
2 tablespoons flour
¼ teaspoon baking powder
¼ teaspoon salt

½ cup flaked coconut
1 (3½-ounce) can (1 cup)
  toasted macadamia nuts,
  coarsely chopped
Powdered sugar for topping

Beat the eggs, vanilla, and brown sugar together until smooth. Sift flour with baking powder and salt; stir into egg mixture and blend well. Fold in coconut and nuts to complete the Filling.

BUTTER CRUST:

½ cup butter
¼ cup sugar

1 cup flour

Blend butter, sugar, and flour together with a fork to make a crumbly texture. Press into a 9-inch-square pan. Bake at 350° for 20 minutes or until light brown. Remove from the oven.

Gently spread Filling over crust. Bake an additional 25 minutes at 350°. Remove from oven and place on a rack. Sprinkle with powdered sugar. Cool 5 minutes, then cut with a knife into desired size squares. For a romantic dessert, serve with chilled champagne!

Honolulu Hawaii Cooking

Calabash Cousins Coconut Bars

Rich with coconut and macadamias, these bars won't last long in your household. They are named after the volunteer support group for the Daughters of Hawai'i who maintain our beloved Hulihe'e Palace.

1½ cups plus 1 tablespoon all-purpose flour, divided
1½ cups firmly packed brown sugar, divided
½ cup butter, softened
2 eggs, beaten

½ teaspoon baking powder
¼ teaspoon salt
½ teaspoon vanilla extract
1¼ cups shredded coconut
½ cup chopped macadamia nuts

Combine 1½ cups flour and ½ cup brown sugar in medium bowl. Cut in butter with 2 knives or pastry cutter until mixture resembles coarse meal. Press into bottom of a lightly greased 9-inch-square pan. Bake in preheated oven at 350° for 15 minutes.

Meanwhile, combine eggs, remaining one cup brown sugar, 1 tablespoon flour, baking powder, salt, and vanilla in large bowl, mixing well. Stir in shredded coconut and chopped macadamia nuts. Spread coconut mixture over crust. Bake at 350° for 20 minutes. Remove and cool. Cut into 2-inch-square bars. Yields 20.

Kona on My Plate

Pineapple Bars

2 cups sugar
½ cup butter, softened
1 (20-ounce) can
  crushed pineapple, drained
1 cup chopped walnuts

1 cup flour
½ teaspoon salt
½ teaspoon baking soda
6 eggs

Mix all ingredients well. Bake in greased 10x15x2-inch pan at 350° for 30–35 minutes. Cut into bars.

We, the Women of Hawaii Cookbook

Pineapple Squares

½ cup (1 stick) butter or
  margarine, softened
1⅓ cups sugar
4 eggs
1½ cups flour
1 teaspoon baking powder

½ teaspoon baking soda
¼ teaspoon salt
1 (20-ounce) can crushed
  pineapple, drained
Powdered sugar

Cream together butter and sugar with an electric mixer for 2 minutes on high speed. Mix in eggs. Add dry ingredients, except the powdered sugar, and mix.

Drain pineapple by pressing the top of the open can against the pineapple while draining the juice. Add pineapple to the ingredients in the bowl and stir with a spoon until blended. Pour batter into a greased, 9x13-inch pan and bake for 30–35 minutes at 350°. Cool; cut into 24 bars. Sprinkle with powdered sugar.

Aunty Pua's Keiki Cookbook

Editor's Extra: Don't throw the pineapple juice away. I like adding it to orange juice.

Mud Slide Brownies

2 cups all-purpose flour
1/2 teaspoon baking powder
1/2 teaspoon salt
2/3 cup unsalted butter
4 ounces unsweetened
   chocolate
3 eggs, beaten

1 1/2 cups sugar
4 tablespoons Kahlúa
2 tablespoons Bailey's Irish
   Cream
1 tablespoon vodka
3/4 cup chopped walnuts

Preheat oven to 350°; lightly grease a 9x13-inch baking pan. On wax paper, sift together dry ingredients. In a saucepan over medium heat, melt butter and chocolate, stirring to blend. Cool. In a mixing bowl, combine eggs and sugar. Stir in dry ingredients, then add chocolate mixture and liqueurs. Stir in nuts. Spread into prepared pan; bake for 25–30 minutes. Serves 12.

Dd's Table Talk

Da Kine Brownies

These brownies are a great finger dessert. Women eat them in two or three bites and most men pop the whole thing in their mouths. For a sophisticated dessert, serve brownie with vanilla ice cream drizzled with a little homemade raspberry sauce. (In Hawaiian slang, "Da Kine" means "the best.")

1 package Betty Crocker's
   Fudge Brownie Mix
1/2 cup unsweetened
   applesauce (instead of oil)

1/3 cup natural peanut butter
1/3 cup semisweet chocolate
   chips

Preheat oven to 325°. According to package directions, blend appropriate amount water and eggs, then applesauce, and peanut butter in a large bowl; add mix. Stir until moistened and fully blended. Add chocolate chips. Spoon batter into Teflon-coated mini-muffin pan without paper inserts. Instead, spray lightly with nonstick cooking spray. Bake for about 20 minutes, depending on oven, or until done. Do not overbake. Allow brownies to cool and pop them out onto a serving tray. Stand back so you won't get trampled.

Shaloha Cookbook

Coffee Glazed Brownies

A delicious treat with a nice cold glass of skim milk for an after-school treat!

1 cup unbleached flour	3 tablespoons canola oil
½ teaspoon baking soda	1 tablespoon applesauce mixed
½ teaspoon baking powder	with 1 tablespoon strong
¼ cup oat bran	coffee
⅓ cup sugar	3 tablespoons light corn syrup
⅓ cup unsweetened cocoa	2 egg whites, lightly beaten
1 large ripe banana, mashed	¼ teaspoon almond extract
well	1 teaspoon vanilla

Preheat oven to 350°. Prepare 8-inch baking pan with cooking spray. Combine flour, baking soda, baking powder, bran, sugar, and cocoa; mix well and set aside. Combine banana, canola oil, applesauce-coffee mixture, corn syrup, egg whites, and extracts; beat for a few minutes and add to dry mixture, combining well. Pour into pan and bake for about 25 minutes, or until center is set.

GLAZE:

½ cup confectioners' sugar	3–4 teaspoons strong coffee
3 teaspoons cocoa	blend

Mix sugar and cocoa. Gradually add coffee until mixture drizzles slowly from spoon. Drizzle Glaze in zig zag pattern over top of warm brownies. Cut into squares when cooled. Makes 12 squares.

Nutritional analysis per serving: Cal 180; Fat 3.5g; Chol 0mg; Sod 85mg

The Best of Heart-y Cooking

Hawai'i is the only state that grows cacao beans used to make chocolate. Cacao is the name of the tree that produces a 6- to 10-inch pod containing 20 to 40 seeds. To become chocolate, the seeds are fermented, dried, aged, lightly roasted, ground, and conched (the process of continuously mixing, grinding, and stirring).

Toll House Bars

1 cup butter, softened
1 cup brown sugar
1 large egg
1 teaspoon vanilla

2 cups flour
6 ounces chocolate chips
1 cup chopped nuts

Cream butter, sugar, and egg; add vanilla and flour; mix well. Stir in chocolate chips and chopped nuts. Preheat oven to 325°. Spread dough on greased 17x14-inch cookie sheet or jellyroll sheet. Roll with rolling pin or pat with hand to 1 inch from edge of pan. Bake for 25 minutes. Cut into 1½-inch bars. Makes about 48 bars.

Favorite Island Cookery Book IV

Chocolate Walnut Crumb Bars

1 cup (2 sticks) butter,
  softened
2 cups all-purpose flour
½ cup sugar
¼ teaspoon salt
2 cups (12-ounce package)
  chocolate chips, divided

1¼ cups (14-ounce can)
  sweetened condensed milk
1 teaspoon vanilla
1 cup chopped walnuts

Preheat oven to 350°. Beat butter in large mixing bowl until creamy. Add flour, sugar, and salt, and mix until crumbly. With floured fingers, press 2 cups crumb mixture onto bottom of greased, 9x13-inch baking pan; reserve remaining mixture. Bake for 10–12 minutes until edges are golden brown.

Warm 1½ cups chocolate chips and sweetened condensed milk in small, heavy saucepan over low heat, stirring until smooth. Stir in vanilla. Spread chocolate mixture over hot crust. Stir walnuts and remaining chocolate chips into reserved crumb mixture; sprinkle over chocolate filling. Bake for 25–30 minutes until center is set. Cool in pan on wire rack. Cut with sharp knife into bars. Makes 24–30.

Kailua Cooks

Mango Bars

CRUST:

2 cups flour	1 cup butter, softened
½ cup sugar	

Preheat oven to 350°. Grease 9x13-inch baking pan. Combine flour with sugar. Add butter and press into prepared baking pan; bake 7 minutes.

FILLING:

4 cups chopped mangoes	1 teaspoon vanilla
¾ cup sugar	1 teaspoon cinnamon
⅓ cup water	3 tablespoons cornstarch
1 teaspoon lemon juice	3 tablespoons water

Combine mangoes, sugar, water, lemon juice, vanilla, and cinnamon in a saucepan. Simmer until the mangoes are tender, about 10 minutes. Combine cornstarch and water; stir into the mango mixture and cook until thickened. Remove from heat and cool slightly. Pour over prepared Crust.

TOPPING:

2 cups quick oats	½ cup sugar
¼ cup flour	⅔ cup butter, softened

Combine oats, flour, and sugar. Blend in butter and sprinkle over mango mixture. Bake for 50 minutes; cool and cut into bars. Store in refrigerator. Makes 2 dozen.

Kailua Cooks

Aloha shirts, or Hawaiian shirts, began their rise to popularity in the 1920s and 1930s. These brightly colored shirts with bold Hawaiian-themed prints actually got their start in the sugar cane and pineapple plantations. To keep cool, plantation workers created the original shirts by combining styles of clothing brought with them from the Philippines, Japan, and China.

Pies and Other Desserts

James Dole paid 1.1 million or $12 an acre for the island of Lana'i in 1922, and planted 16,000 acres of pineapples there. Today more than one-third of the world's commercial supply of pineapples comes from Hawai'i.

Fresh Mango Pie

For mango pie, you can use pretty ripe mangoes. If you prefer tart pies, use mangoes that are less ripe and add the juice from half a lemon.

4 cups mango slices	1 teaspoon cinnamon
1 teaspoon lemon juice	Pastry for (8-inch) 2-crust pie
½ cup sugar	1 tablespoon butter or
3 tablespoons cornstarch	margarine

Put all ingredients except pastry and butter in a bowl and mix them gently. Line a pie pan with half the pastry. Pour mango filling into the pastry and dot with butter. Cover pie with top crust. Crimp edges and slit crust to allow steam to escape. Bake pie at 400° for about 45 minutes or until crust is golden brown and juice is bubbly.

Kau Kau Kitchen

Guava Chiffon Pie

4 eggs	1 package unflavored gelatin
½ cup sugar, divided	¼ cup water
¼ teaspoon salt	1 tablespoon lemon juice
1¼ cups frozen guava	1 9-inch pie shell, baked
concentrate, divided	Whipped cream for garnish

Separate eggs. Beat egg yolks until light. Add ¼ cup sugar, ¼ teaspoon salt, and ½ cup guava concentrate. Cook mixture in top of double boiler until smooth and thickened slightly, stirring continually. Soak gelatin in water to soften and add to hot mixture. Remove from heat and cool to room temperature. Add lemon juice and remainder of guava concentrate. Chill until partly set.

Whip egg whites until stiffened. Add remaining ¼ cup sugar slowly while continually beating. Whip partly set gelatin mixture and fold in egg whites. Pour into pie shell and top with whipped cream.

Hawai'i's Island Cooking

Macadamia Nut Pie

¼ pound (1 stick) butter,
softened
¾ cup sugar
3 eggs, slightly beaten
¾ cup dark corn syrup

¼ teaspoon salt
1 teaspoon vanilla
1 cup chopped, unsalted
macadamia nuts
1 unbaked pie shell

Cream butter; add sugar gradually. When light and lemon colored, add the beaten eggs. Blend in corn syrup. Add salt, vanilla, and nuts. Mix well, then pour into the unbaked pie shell. Bake in a 350° oven for 35–40 minutes.

Joys of Hawaiian Cooking

Haupia Pie

1 (10- to 12-ounce) can
coconut milk
¼ cup sugar
¼ cup water

3 tablespoons cornstarch
1 (8-inch) prepared graham
cracker crust

Put coconut milk and sugar in saucepan and heat. Measure water in a liquid measuring cup and add the cornstarch to it. Stir until smooth and add to the hot coconut milk. Cook on medium heat until mixture thickens, stirring constantly. Cool to room temperature and pour into prepared crust. Refrigerate at least 3 hours. Serves 6.

Aunty Pua's Keiki Cookbook

 There are only twelve letters in the Hawaiian Alphabet:
Vowels: A, E, I, O, U
Consonants: H, K, L, M, N, P, W

Liliko'i Pistachio Pie

CRUST:

3 cups flour
3½ tablespoons sugar
1⅛ teaspoons salt

1 cup oil
3⅓ tablespoons milk

Mix all together. Press in 9x13-inch pan. Prick shell. Bake at 325° for 45 minutes until golden brown. Cool.

FIRST LAYER:

1½ cups powdered sugar, sifted
2 (8-ounce) packages cream cheese, softened

2 cups Cool Whip

Beat sugar and cream cheese. Stir in Cool Whip. Spread on Crust. Refrigerate until set.

SECOND LAYER:

2 (3¾-ounce) boxes pistachio instant pudding

Follow pudding directions on box label. Spread over First Layer. Refrigerate.

THIRD LAYER:

2 packages unflavored gelatin
½ cup cold water
6 eggs, separated

1⅓ cups sugar, divided
1 cup fresh liliko'i (passion fruit) juice

Soak gelatin in water. Beat egg yolks until light. Add 1 cup sugar and continue beating until light. Cook in double boiler, stirring continuously until thick. Remove from heat; add soft gelatin. Beat and cool to room temperature. Add liliko'i juice. Chill to partly set. Whip egg whites until stiff. Add remaining ⅓ cup sugar slowly while beating. Fold into whipped gelatin. Spread over Second Layer.

TOPPING:

1 (8-ounce) container Cool Whip

Finely chopped macadamia nuts, for sprinkling

Spread Cool Whip over Third Layer. Sprinkle with nuts.

Hawai'i's Best Local Desserts

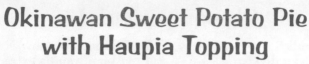

Okinawan Sweet Potato Pie with Haupia Topping

A new favorite that combines the different textures of a light crust, dense sweet potato, and smooth haupia. A hands-down winner at any gathering.

CRUST:

4 tablespoons sugar
1½ cups flour
½ cup chopped nuts (optional)

¾ cup margarine or butter
(1½ sticks)

Combine sugar, flour, and nuts. Cut margarine into flour mixture until texture is sandy. Press lightly into 9x13-inch pan. Bake at 325° for 20–25 minutes.

FILLING:

8 tablespoons butter or
margarine, softened
1 cup sugar
2 eggs, beaten
2 cups Okinawan sweet potato,
cooked and mashed

½ cup evaporated milk
1 teaspoon vanilla
¼ teaspoon salt

Beat butter and sugar. Add eggs and mix. Gradually mix in mashed sweet potatoes. Add evaporated milk, vanilla, and salt; mix well. Pour onto Crust. Bake at 350° for 30–35 minutes. Cool.

HAUPIA TOPPING:

½ cup sugar
½ cup cornstarch
1½ cups water

2 (12-ounce) cans frozen
coconut milk, thawed

Combine sugar and cornstarch; stir in water and blend well. Stir sugar mixture into coconut milk; cook and stir over low heat until thickened. Cool slightly. Pour coconut milk mixture (haupia) over the pie filling and refrigerate.

Hawai'i's Best Local Desserts

The Okinawan sweet potato has a unique dark purple color and a dry texture and sweet flavor, making it unlike other types of sweet potatoes. Purple sweet potatoes contain a high fiber level.

Coconut Cream Pie

2 cups milk
1 cup sugar, divided
¼ teaspoon salt
¼ cup grated coconut
4 egg yolks
3 tablespoons cornstarch

1 tablespoon butter
1 teaspoon vanilla extract
2 drops almond extract
1 (9-inch) pie shell, baked
Sweetened whipped cream
(optional)

Combine milk, ½ cup sugar, salt, and coconut in double boiler, and heat to near boiling. Mix together egg yolks, remaining ½ cup sugar, and cornstarch; add to milk mixture and cook until thickened. Add butter, vanilla, and almond extract. Cool and pour into baked pie shell. Top with whipped cream and additional coconut, if desired. Serves 6–8.

The Tastes and Tales of Moiliili

Frozen Lemon Pie

2 eggs, separated
⅓ cup lemon juice
Grated rind of ½ lemon

½ cup sugar, divided
1 cup whipped cream
½ cup cookie crumbs, divided

Beat egg yolks; add lemon juice, rind, and all but 2 tablespoons of sugar. Cook over low heat, stirring constantly for 15 minutes; cool. Beat egg whites until stiff; add remaining sugar. Fold into egg yolk mixture and mix. Beat cream and fold into mixture.

Line a 9-inch pan with wax paper. Sprinkle some crumbs on paper and add lemon mixture. Shake more crumbs on top. Cover with wax paper and freeze. Keeps well in the freezer.

Hilo Woman's Club Cookbook

Kona Coffee Ice Cream Pie

3 pints vanilla ice cream
1½ cups heavy cream, divided
½ cup coarsely chopped
  macadamia nuts
2 tablespoons coffee liqueur
2 tablespoons instant coffee

1 (9-inch) pastry shell, baked
4 egg whites
¼ teaspoon cream of tartar
½ cup sugar
Maraschino cherries for
  garnish

Soften 1 pint ice cream in a medium-size bowl. Beat ½ of the heavy cream in a small bowl until stiff. Fold into softened ice cream along with nuts and liqueur. If very soft, place in freezer until mixture holds its shape.

Soften remaining 2 pints ice cream in large bowl. Stir instant coffee into remaining heavy cream. Beat until stiff. Fold into remaining softened ice cream. Spread ⅔ coffee mixture in pastry shell. Make a depression in center. Spoon macadamia mixture into center. Mound remaining coffee mixture on top. Freeze overnight or until firm.

Beat egg whites and cream of tartar until foamy. Beat in sugar until meringue forms soft peaks. Cover ice cream filling with meringue and maraschino cherries in proportions desired. Chill.

Hawaii–Cooking with Aloha

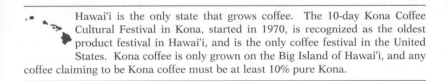

Hawai'i is the only state that grows coffee. The 10-day Kona Coffee Cultural Festival in Kona, started in 1970, is recognized as the oldest product festival in Hawai'i, and is the only coffee festival in the United States. Kona coffee is only grown on the Big Island of Hawai'i, and any coffee claiming to be Kona coffee must be at least 10% pure Kona.

Pineapple Bread Pudding

Most bread puddings call for whole eggs and milk, which is the source of lots of fat and calories. Pineapple packed in its' own juice adds to the flavor without the calories of heavy sugar syrups, so you can enjoy the taste without the guilt.

6 slices whole-wheat bread,
  lightly toasted and cut
  into cubes
¼ cup chopped dates
¼ cup golden raisins
1 (8-ounce) can crushed
  pineapple, drained
1 egg
2 egg whites

½ cup sugar
⅓ cup water
1 teaspoon vanilla
½ teaspoon nutmeg
½ teaspoon cinnamon
1 (13-ounce) can evaporated
  skim milk
Cinnamon sugar to sprinkle on
  top

Preheat oven to 350°. Spray 8x8-inch pan with cooking spray. Place half of the bread on bottom of baking pan. Sprinkle with chopped dates and raisins and spread crushed pineapple over all; cover with remaining bread. Beat egg and egg whites with sugar until frothy; add in water until blended. Add vanilla, spices, and milk, and beat until mixed well. Pour over bread mixture; sprinkle cinnamon sugar on top. Bake for about 40 minutes, or until center tests dry. Remove from oven and cool on wire rack. Cut into squares. Makes 9 servings.

Nutritional analysis per serving: Cal 175; Fat 2g; Chol 30mg; Sod 160mg

The Best of Heart-y Cooking

The Pineapple Garden Maze at the Dole Plantation was the "World's Largest Maze," according to The Guinness Book of World Records 2001. You can spend half an hour or half a day among its 1.7 miles of paths.

Lemon Pudding

1 cup sugar
⅛ teaspoon salt
¼ cup flour
2 tablespoons margarine,
  melted

4–5 tablespoons lemon juice
1 tablespoon grated lemon peel
2 egg yolks, well beaten
1 cup milk, scalded
2 egg whites, stiffly beaten

Combine sugar, salt, flour, and melted margarine. Add lemon juice and peel. Stir in well-beaten egg yolks and scalded milk. Mix well. Fold in beaten egg whites; pour into a greased, 1½-quart casserole. Bake in larger pan with 1 inch of hot water for 1 hour in 325° oven. Sponge cake comes to top, and layer of lemon custard forms on bottom.

Note: If it curdles, it will be all right after baking.

Hawaii Cooks Throughout the Year

Haupia
(Coconut Pudding)

2 cups boiling water
6 cups grated coconut
  (2 coconuts)

3 or 6 tablespoons cornstarch
  (for soft or firm pudding)
3½ tablespoons sugar

Pour boiling water over coconut and allow to stand for 15 minutes. Strain through double thickness of cheesecloth, squeezing out as much of the milk as possible, about 3 cups. If not 3 cups, add milk poured from the coconut to equal 3 cups. Mix cornstarch (appropriate amount) with sugar and add sufficient coconut milk to make a smooth paste. Heat remaining milk to boiling and slowly stir in cornstarch paste. Boil until it thickens. Pour into mold and allow to cool. Cut into squares and serve on squares of ti leaves.

Joys of Hawaiian Cooking

Haupia Coconut Pudding

3 tablespoons cornstarch
3 tablespoons sugar

½ teaspoon salt
2 cups coconut milk, divided

Combine dry ingredients. Add ½ cup of coconut milk and blend to a smooth paste. Heat remaining milk on low heat. Add cornstarch mixture, stirring constantly until thickened. Pour into shallow pan. Let it cool until firm. Yields 6 servings.

The Friends of 'Iolani Palace Cookbook

Mango Dessert

CRUST:
1½ sticks margarine,
   softened

2 cups flour
⅓ cup sugar

Mix softened margarine and flour; add sugar and mix well. Press in 9x13-inch pan and bake at 350° till lightly brown (10 minutes or so). Set aside.

FILLING:
2 packages unflavored gelatin
1 cup water
1 cup hot water
¼ teaspoon salt
1 cup sugar

2 drops yellow food coloring
4 tablespoons lemon juice
4 cups sliced mangoes
1 (8-ounce) carton Cool Whip

Soften gelatin in cold water. Add hot water, salt, sugar, and food coloring. Mix. Add lemon juice and let cool. When it has congealed, add mangoes. Pour over Crust and refrigerate until firm. Cover with Cool Whip.

A Lei of Recipes

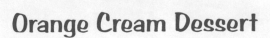

Orange Cream Dessert

CRUST:

¾ cup (1½ sticks) margarine
¼ cup firmly packed brown
 sugar

1½ cups flour
½ cup chopped nuts

Cream margarine and sugar. Add flour and nuts; mix well. Spread dough in 9x13-inch pan and bake at 375° for 10 minutes. Cool.

FILLING:

1 (8-ounce) package cream
 cheese, softened
¾ cup sugar or 1 cup
 powdered sugar

1 (4-ounce) carton Cool Whip

Beat cream cheese and sugar. Fold in Cool Whip. Spread Filling evenly on Crust. Chill for ½ hour.

TOPPING:

1 envelope unflavored gelatin
1 cup cold water, divided
1 (6-ounce) package orange
 Jell-O

2 cups hot water
1 pint orange sherbet
2 (11-ounce) cans Mandarin
 oranges, drained

Soften unflavored gelatin in ¼ cup water and set aside. In large bowl, dissolve Jell-O with hot water; add softened gelatin and remaining water and stir until dissolved. Fold in sherbet and Mandarin oranges. Pour Jell-O mixture over cream cheese mixture and refrigerate.

Friends and Celebrities Cookbook II

In 1978, Hawaiian was made an official language of the state of Hawai'i. In 1990, the United States government established a policy recognizing the right of Hawai'i to preserve, use, and support its indigenous language. Hawai'i is the only state to officially recognize a native language.

Kona Coffee Chocolate Pôt de Crème

12 ounces Hawaiian semisweet
  chocolate, finely chopped
2 large eggs
½ teaspoon salt
1½ cups fresh milk
1 tablespoon Irish cream or
  other liqueur

3 tablespoons instant Kona
  coffee
Whipped cream and chocolate
  shavings (optional)

Place first 3 ingredients in blender container. Scald together milk and liqueur over medium-high heat, stirring constantly. Remove from heat and stir in Kona coffee granules until dissolved. Add hot liquid to blender and immediately blend all ingredients for 5–8 seconds at high speed. Divide mixture among 8 small dessert ramekins or pôt de crème cups and chill until firm, at least 4 hours. Serve unadorned in traditional manner, or garnish with a dollop of slightly sweetened whipped cream and shaved chocolate. Almost any liqueur of choice is suitable for taste variations. Serves 8.

Kona on My Plate

Academy Café Chocolate Sauce

One of the loveliest spots in Honolulu to lunch is the courtyard restaurant at the Honolulu Academy of Arts.

1 (16-ounce) can chocolate
  fudge topping
8 ounces chocolate syrup
½ teaspoon cinnamon

Salt to taste
4 tablespoons Kahlúa liqueur
  or crème de cacao
Candied ginger for topping

In a medium bowl, mix all the ingredients (except ginger) together until well blended. Refrigerate until ready to serve. Serve on vanilla ice cream with chopped candied ginger.

Hawaiian Country Tables

Mai Tai Sundae Sauce

1 (12-ounce) jar pineapple-
  mango jam, or peach jam
3 tablespoons butter
2 teaspoons lime juice

¼ cup orange marmalade
½ teaspoon each: cinnamon,
  cloves, and nutmeg
¼ cup rum

Combine all ingredients, except rum. Cook over low heat until smoothly blended. Add rum. Serve warm over ice cream (macadamia flavor is best). Bananas may also be added just before serving.

The Friends of 'Iolani Palace Cookbook

Famous Hawaiians include Tia Carrere, Don Ho, Kelly Hu, Jack Johnson, Nicole Kidman, Jason Scott Lee, Bruno Mars, Bette Midler, Barack Obama, Kelly Preston, Harold Sakata, James Shigeta, Don Stroud, Manti Te'o, and Michelle Wie.

Vanilla Coconut Ball Treats

1½ cups sweetened coconut
shreds
1 stick butter
1 cup condensed milk

1 large Symphony candy bar
Vanilla ice cream
Chopped nuts (optional)

Brown coconut shreds under broiler until golden brown. Set aside and cool. Melt butter, then add milk and chocolate bar a piece at a time, and heat slowly until the consistency is creamy. Make ice cream into balls and roll in coconut shreds. Top each ball with chocolate sauce; serve immediately. Nuts of your choice can be added to the top of each vanilla ball, if desired.

Recipe by Fire Fighter 3 Brian Derby
Hawai'i's Favorite Firehouse Recipes

Contributors

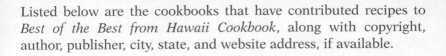

Listed below are the cookbooks that have contributed recipes to *Best of the Best from Hawaii Cookbook*, along with copyright, author, publisher, city, state, and website address, if available.

Another Taste of Aloha ©1993 The Junior League of Honolulu, HI, www.juniorleagueofhonolulu.org

Aunty Pua's Keiki Cookbook ©1991 by Ann Kondo Corum, Bess Press, Honolulu, HI, www.besspress.com

The Best of Heart-y Cooking, by Diana Helfand, Kailua, HI

Burst of Flavor: The Fine Art of Cooking with Spices ©2001 by Kusuma Cooray, University of Hawaii Press, Honolulu, HI, www.uhpress.hawaii.edu

Classic Cookbook Recipes, by Christine Mayural, Waipahu, HI

Cook 'em up Kaua'i ©1993 Kauai Historical Society, Lihue, HI, www.kauaihistoricalsociety.org

Cooking Italian in Hawaii ©1991 by George Sabato "Cass" Castagnola, Watermark Publishing, Honolulu, HI

Dd's Table Talk, by Deirdre Kieko Todd, www.ddstabletalk.com, Booklines Hawaii, Ltd., Mililani, HI, www.booklineshawaii.com

Dd's Table Talk II, by Deirdre Kieko Todd, www.ddstabletalk.com, Booklines Hawaii, Ltd., Mililani, HI, www.booklineshawaii.com

Eat More, Weigh Less™ Cookbook ©1995 by Terry Shintani, M.D., J.D., M.P.H., Hawaii Health Foundation, Honolulu, HI

Ethnic Foods of Hawai'i ©2000 by Ann Kondo Corum, Bess Press, Honolulu, HI, www.besspress.com

Favorite Island Cookery Book I, Honpa Hongwanji Hawaii Betsuin, Honolulu, HI

Favorite Island Cookery Book II, Honpa Hongwanji Hawaii Betsuin, Honolulu, HI

Favorite Island Cookery Book III, Honpa Hongwanji Hawaii Betsuin, Honolulu, HI

Favorite Island Cookery Book IV, Honpa Hongwanji Hawaii Betsuin, Honolulu, HI

Favorite Island Cookery Book V, Honpa Hongwanji Hawaii Betsuin, Honolulu, HI

Favorite Island Cookery Book VI, Honpa Hongwanji Hawaii Betsuin, Honolulu, HI

Favorite Recipes for Islanders, Hilo Extension Homemakers Council, Inc., Betty Jo Thompson, Hilo, HI

Fresh Catch of the Day...from the Fishwife, by Shirley Rizzuto, Hawaii Fishing News, Honolulu, HI, www.hawaiifishingnews.com

Friends and Celebrities Cookbook II, Castle Performing Arts Center, Kaneohe, HI

The Friends of 'Iolani Palace Cookbook ©1987 The Friends of 'Iolani Palace, Honolulu, HI, www.iolanipalace.org

Hawaii–Cooking with Aloha ©1981, 1984 by Elvira Monroe, Gertrude Margah, Theoni Pappas (by Elvira Monroe and Irish Margah), Wide World Publishing, San Carlos, CA, www.wideworld-publishing.com

Hawaii Cooks Throughout the Year ©1990 by Maili Yardley, Editions Limited, Honolulu, HI, editionslimited@hawaii.rr.com

Hawai'i Tropical Rum Drinks & Cuisine ©2001 Mutual Publishing, by Arnold Bitner and Phoebe Beach, Mutual Publishing, Honolulu, HI, www.mutualpublishing.com

Hawaiian Country Tables ©1998 The Bess Press, Inc., by Kaui Philpotts, Bess Press, Honolulu, HI 96816, www.besspress.com

Hawai'i's Best Local Desserts ©2001 Mutual Publishing, by Jean Watanabe Hee, Mutual Publishing, Honolulu, HI , www.mutualpublishing.com

Hawai'i's Best Local Dishes ©2002 Mutual Publishing, by Jean Watanabe Hee, Mutual Publishing, Honolulu, HI, www.mutualpublishing.com

Hawai'i's Best Mochi Recipes ©2000 Mutual Publishing, by Jean Watanabe Hee, Mutual Publishing, Honolulu, HI, www.mutualpublishing.com

Hawaii's Best Tropical Food & Drinks, Hawaiian Service Inc., a division of Booklines Hawaii, Ltd., Mililani, HI, www.booklines-hawaii.com

Hawai'i's Favorite Firehouse Recipes ©2002 FilmWorks Press, Honolulu, HI, www.filmworkspa-cific.com

Hawai'i's Favorite Pineapple Recipes ©2002 Mutual Publishing, by Joannie Dobbs and Betty Shimabukuro, Mutual Publishing, Honolulu, HI, www.mutualpublishing.com

Hawai'i's Island Cooking ©1996 Mutual Publishing, by Bonnie Tuell, Mutual Publishing, Honolulu, HI, www.mutualpub-lishing.com

Hawai'i's Spam™ Cookbook ©1987 by Ann Kondo Corum, Bess Press, Honolulu, HI, www.besspress.com

Hawai'i's 2nd Spam™ Cookbook ©2001 by Ann Kondo Corum, Bess Press, Honolulu, HI, www.besspress.com

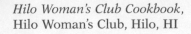

Hilo Woman's Club Cookbook, Hilo Woman's Club, Hilo, HI

Honolulu Hawaii Cooking by Betty Evans, Hermosa Beach, CA

How to Use Hawaiian Fruit ©1974 Petroglyph Press, by Agnes Alexander, Petroglyph Press, Hilo, HI, www.basically-books.com

Incredibly Delicious: Recipes for a New Paradigm ©2003 Gentle World Inc., Kapa'au, HI, www.gentleworld.org

Island Flavors, Historic Hawaii Foundation, Honolulu, HI, www.historichawaii.org

Joys of Hawaiian Cooking ©1977 Petroglyph Press, by Martin and Judy Beeman, Petroglyph

Kailua Cooks: Hana Hou ©2002 Le Jardin Academy, Island Heritage Publishing, Kailua, HI, www.lejardinacademy.com

Kau Kau Kitchen ©1986 by Dana Black, Press Pacifica, Ltd., Kailua, HI

Kona On My Plate ©2002 Kona Outdoor Circle Foundation, Kailua-Kona, HI, www.konacook-book.com

A Lei of Recipes, Kauai Association for Family and Community Education, Lihue, HI

Paradise Preserves ©1987 by Yvonne Neely Armitage, by Yvonne Hodgins, Press Pacifica, Ltd., Kailua, HI

Pupus–An Island Tradition ©1995 The Bess Press, Inc., by Sachi Fukuda, Bess Press, Honolulu, HI, www.besspress.com

Pupus from Paradise, Assistance League of Hawaii, Honolulu, HI, www.kokuawithaloha.org

A Race for Life ©2000 by Ruth Heidrich, Ph. D., Lantern Books, Honolulu, HI, www.ruthhei-drich.com

Sam Choy's Sampler ©2000 by Chef Sam Choy, Mutual Publishing, Honolulu, HI, www.mutualpublishing.com

Seasoned with Aloha Vol. 2, VP-9 Officer Spouses' Club, Kailua, HI

Shaloha Cookbook ©2002 Congregation Kona Beth Shalom, Kailua-Kona, HI , klimes@aloha.net

The Shoreline Chef: Creative Cuisine for Hawaiian Reef Fish ©2003 by Elmer Guzman, Watermark Publishing, Honolulu, HI, www.book-shawaii.net

Sugar and Spice–Cookies Made with Love, by Kelimia Mednick, Honolulu, HI

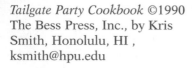

Tailgate Party Cookbook ©1990 The Bess Press, Inc., by Kris Smith, Honolulu, HI , ksmith@hpu.edu

A Taste of Aloha ©1983 The Junior League of Honolulu, HI, www.juniorleagueofhonolulu.org

The Tastes and Tales of Moiliili, Moiliili Community Center, Honolulu, HI

Tropical Taste ©2001 by Sonia Martinez, Honomu, HI, cuban-wahine@hawaii.rr.com

Unbearably Good! Mochi Lovers' Cookbook, by Teresa DeVirgilio-Lam, Honolulu, HI

Vegetarian Nights by Bonnie Mandoe Gusto, Las Cruces, NM

We, the Women of Hawaii Cookbook ©1986 We, the Women of Hawaii, Press Pacifica, Inc., Kailua, HI

West Kauai's Plantation Heritage ©2002 West Kauai Community Development Corporation, Waimea, HI, www.waimea-plantation.com/shop

The haleakala silversword grows only in the crater and outer slopes of Haleakala Volcano, within Haleakala National Park, Maui, Hawai'i. The silversword matures from seed to its final flowering stage any time from 15 to 50 years. It flowers only once and then dies.

Index

Index

Index

173

Collect the Series!

Recipe Hall of Fame Cookbook Collection

The Recipe Hall of Fame Cookbook

The Recipe Hall of Fame Cookbook II

Quick & Easy Cookbook

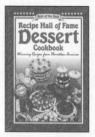

Dessert Cookbook

Dessert Cookbook

One-Dish Wonders

Southern Recipes

Family Favorites

To order by credit card, call toll-free **1-800-343-1583**, visit **www.quailridge.com**, or use the Order Form below. Be sure to mention **Collect the Series** special discount.

Ⓠ Order Form

Send check, money order, or credit card info to:
QUAIL RIDGE PRESS • P. O. Box 123 • Brandon, MS 39043

Name _____

Address _____

City _____

State/Zip _____

Phone # _____

Email Address _____

❑ Check enclosed

Charge to: ❑ Visa ❑ MC ❑ AmEx ❑ Disc

Card # _____

Expiration Date _____

Signature _____

Qty.	Title of Book (or State) (or Set)	Total

Subtotal _____

Mississippi residents add 7% sales tax _____

Postage (any number of books) + $5.00

TOTAL _____